Guideposts to Meaning

Discovering What Really Matters

by Joseph Fabry

An Institute of Logoth

D1069336

Copyright © 1988 by
Joseph Fabry

Published by New Harbinger Publications
5674 Shattuck Ave.
Oakland, CA 94609

All rights reserved
Printed in the United States of America

Approximately 20 percent of this text
is a translation of material in
the author's previous work
Wege zur Selbstfindung,
published by Herder Verlag,
Hermann Herder Strasse,
D-7800 Freiburg,
West Germany

First printing July 1988, 5,000 copies

Acknowledgment

I wish to acknowledge my gratitude to a number of logotherapists who have found new practical applications of Dr. Viktor Frankl's ideas, on which this book is based. Among them are Elisabeth Lukas, Ph.D., director of the South German Institute of Logotherapy in Munich; Mignon Eisenberg, Ph.D., regional director of the Institute of Logotherapy in Chicago; James Crumbaugh, regional director of the Institute of Logotherapy in Biloxi; James Yoder, regional director of the Institute of Logotherapy in Kansas City; Robert Leslie, Ph.D., curator of the Viktor Frankl Library in Berkeley; Hiroshi Takashima, M.D., director of the Japan Society of Humanistic Anthropology in Tokyo; and John Quirk, logotherapists in Vancouver, British Columbia.

I also wish to thank Carroll Talpers for her many editorial suggestions, and Hyman Roudman for his careful reading of the manuscript.

Joseph Fabry

Contents

Chapter One

Rx: A Search for Meaning

There are two types of people: those who say yes to life in spite of their setbacks, and those who say no to life in spite of the good things that happen to them. The yes-people usually feel fulfilled and happy; the no-people usually feel alienated, frustrated, empty.

Like most people, you probably fall between these extremes. You have acquired your attitude from experiences in childhood and later in life, and from role models and teachings. Your attitude may have shifted during your life. It is important to realize that you *can* shift from a negative to a positive attitude. If you are a no-sayer, that does not mean that you are destined to remain a no-sayer. Some people have been helped in this shift by religion, others by philosophy, and—recently—some by psychology.

Psychology is a young science. During most of its hundred years of existence, psychology has been concerned with curing those who are ill. The Viennese psychiatrist Viktor Frankl was the first to pay attention also to those who are healthy, to preventing them from becoming ill, frustrated, desperate. Frankl developed his ideas in the 1930s, and tested those ideas during two and a half years in German concentration camps. When Frankl was freed in 1945, he wrote a book, *Say Yes to Life in Spite of Everything*. Under the title *Man's Search for Meaning*, that book has sold three million copies in the United States. It has been translated into more than twenty languages and has brought hope and comfort to many people.

Frankl believes that the key to a positive view of life is awareness that life has meaning under all circumstances, and that you have the capacity to find meaning in your life. You can rise above ill health and blows of fate if you see meaning in your existence. Frankl calls his system "logotherapy"— health through meaning. Logotherapy helps people say yes to life, whether the suffering they experience comes from difficult human relations, job trouble, illness, guilt, or death of a loved one, or from self-made problems such as hypochondria or an overwhelming hunger for power, material things, or pleasure.

This book describes the practical applications of logotherapy. It is written, not for the mentally ill, but for the mentally searching. The ideas presented here can be used by members of the caring professions—psychologists, counselors, social workers, ministers, nurses, teachers—and also by lay readers to help family members, friends, or themselves. Finding meaning is the surest way to overcome alienation, doubt, despair, emptiness, and the feeling that you fall short of your potential. Meaning will help you to move toward becoming a yes-sayer. If you decide to seek meaning in your life, you will face three questions:

- What is this meaning you are seeking?
- How can you find it?
- Where can you find it?

What Is Meaning?

Meaning occurs on two levels: ultimate meaning, and the meaning of the moment.

When you seek ultimate meaning, you are aware—even when you face confusion—that there is order in the universe and you are part of that order. If you are religious, you will see this order as divine. If you are a humanist, you may see it in terms of laws of nature and ethics. If you are a scientist, you will see order in the laws of physics, chemistry, astronomy, evolution. If you are an artist, you may see it in harmony. If you are ecology minded, you may see it in balance in the ecosystem.

Ultimate meaning—THE meaning of life—is inaccessible to you. It is like the horizon—you can strive toward it, but you will never reach it. Yet, to be a yes-sayer, you have to pursue ultimate meaning, even if you can never attain it. In fact, if you could attain it and could truthfully say "I know the meaning of life," you would be spiritually dead, because there would be nothing left to strive toward. Ultimate meaning is a matter of faith, of assumption, of personal experience. You can live as if life has meaning and you are part of the web of life; or you can live as if life is chaotic and you are a victim of its whims.

You may find it discouraging to read that life has meaning but that you can never reach it. Fortunately there is a second level of meaning that you can and, indeed, must reach to lead a fulfilled existence. This is what Frankl calls the "meaning of the moment."

Frankl stipulates that you are a unique individual who goes through life in a series of unique situations, and that each moment offers a meaning to fulfill—a chance to act in a meaningful way. This can be achieved through what you do, what you experience, but also through the stands you take in situations of unavoidable tragedy. The unique contribution of logotherapy to mental health is that it enables you to be a yes-sayer in the face of tragedy, to find meaning in meaningless situations.

There is a link between ultimate meaning and the meaning of the moment. If you are aware of ultimate meaning, in either a religious or a secular context, you will be able to respond meaningfully to the offerings of the moment because you have a built-in compass that points toward meaning. If you are not aware of ultimate meaning, you will respond to the meaning of the moment as best you can, and in the course of your life you will gradually approach understanding of ultimate meaning.

How To Find Meaning

Some philosophers, such as the French existentialists Sartre and Camus, maintain that life has no meaning but that human beings need to lead meaningful lives; therefore you *give* your life the meaning you choose. The German existentialists, including Viktor Frankl, assert that meaning exists, and you have to *discover* it. If you could give yourself meaning by making decisions, Frankl says, life would be a meaningless blotch, like a Rorschach test into which you project any meaning you want. Frankl sees life as a puzzle with a hidden picture—like a line drawing of trees, clouds, flowers, and houses, with a caption that says: "Find the bicycle in this picture." You have to turn the drawing this way and that until you discover the bicycle hidden in the confusion of lines. You have to turn life this way and that until you discover meaning. Meaning cannot be given to you by society or your parents. Nor can a psychiatrist *pre*scribe it like a pill. He or she may *de*scribe meaningful responses to your situation, but it is up to you to discover what is meaningful to you.

How can you know which of the many possibilities offered by a particular moment is meaningful to you?

You can't be certain. But with help you can find what is most meaningful to you. Although you have never been in the specific situation you are in now, millions of people over thousands of years have gone through similar situations and found meaningful responses. From those we have distilled values—universal meanings.

Most values change slowly, some fundamental ones not at all. In ordinary situations it is meaningful to follow the values of your culture. Such values are anchored in religious commandments, secular laws, customs, common-sense rules, and the wisdom of some thinkers—for example, Kant's categorical imperative, Gandhi's passive resistance, or Schweitzer's reverence for life.

Today values are in transition. More and more people are unable to find meaning in following traditional values blindly. They reject universal meanings. Children reject the values of their parents, women those of a male-dominated society, church members the dictates of their churches, citizens the laws of governments. People eagerly use their freedom to reject traditional values. But they are less eager to try to find personal responses to the meaning offerings of the moment. They are not willing or able to find such responses. If you reject traditional values, you have to replace them with personal meanings or chaos will result. Values and personal meanings are not moralistic rules, but prescriptions for health. The consequences of irresponsibly created meanings may be neurosis, depression, and suicide.

Today's dilemma is this: Following traditional values may violate your personal sense of meaning. Finding your own path may lead to irresponsible excesses. How can you recognize and respond to the meanings offered by the moment?

Frankl's answer—that you should follow your conscience as you search for meaning—is nothing new in religion and philosophy. It *is* new in medicine, where conscience is disregarded, and in traditional psychotherapy, where it is considered "superego," the result of parental and societal influences from outside the individual.

Logotherapy views conscience as highly personal, as a sort of divining rod that helps you find special meaning in each special situation. Conscience is greatly influenced by society. But you do have the freedom to follow your inner voice, even to reject societal values. As a rule of thumb you can say: "To find the meaning of the moment, I ordinarily follow my cultural values, but in special circumstances I can take the responsibility and follow my conscience."

The voice of conscience is specifically human and thus—like everything human—can err. But it is your only personal guide. You can never be sure if it counsels you correctly. As Gordon Allport expressed it, you "can be half-sure and yet wholehearted." It is a major task of logotherapy to sharpen the inner ear, to make it more alert to the voice of conscience. Some exercises in this book serve that purpose.

Where To Find Meaning

Meaning is everywhere, but you become aware of it only if you tune in on it. It's like the music you hear on the radio: the air is full of sound waves, but you can hear them only when you have a receiver.

Logotherapy research has established that you have a receiver for tuning in meaning. Frankl has called the human spirit our instrument for finding meaning. You have to become aware that you have it, what it contains, and how you can use it.

The human spirit is your specifically human dimension and contains abilities other creatures do not have. Every human is spiritual; in fact, spirit is the essence of being human. You *have* a body that may become ill; you *have* a psyche that may become disturbed. But the spirit is what you *are*. It is your healthy core.

Like the psyche, the spirit is invisible. But there is a difference between psyche and spirit. In the psyche you are driven, by emotions, instinct, needs. In the spirit you are the driver. You make the decisions about what to do with your motivations, with the gifts and handicaps of your body, with the circumstances in which you find yourself. The spirit is the area of human freedom, but also of human responsibility. To lead a fulfilled life, you must be aware that you have this spiritual treasure chest within you, and you must make use of its contents.

Resources of the Human Spirit

The human spirit could also be called the medicine chest of logotherapy. As with all medicines, you must realize that they exist, and then you must learn to use them. They are free and only wait, inside you, to be used. Here are some of the resources of the human spirit:

Will to Meaning

This is the strongest motivation to living and acting. Humans are beings in search of meaning. Seeing meaning in your life enables you to develop your capacities and endure hardships. The founder of psychotherapy, Sigmund Freud, considered the desire for pleasure to be the highest motivational force. Freud's student Alfred Adler (who was Frankl's teacher) considered the desire for power to be our strongest incentive. Both are important: you do act to find pleasure and to achieve power. But, according to Frankl, pleasure is not a primary goal. It is a by-product of having done something meaningful. Power is not an end in itself, but only a means to an end that is attained by using power in a meaningful way. Meaning is neither a by-product nor a means to an end. Meaning is the ultimate goal. If your will to meaning is ignored or repressed, you feel empty.

Task Orientation

To lead a full life, you need tasks waiting for you, both short-term and long-term tasks. They need to be self-chosen, not forced on you (although you may freely agree to a task that is given to you). Commitment to a task helps pull you out of neuroses and depressions, sustains you during difficult periods, and prevents relapses. The curative value of a task is greatest when you feel that only you can accomplish it, or that you are the best one to do it.

Conscience

This is the compass needle that points in the direction of the meaning of the moment. The voice of the conscience is feeble and often drowned out, but your ability to hear it and follow it can alleviate mental anguish and conflict.

Self-Transcendence

This is the ability to reach beyond yourself, toward other people to love and toward causes to make your own. Self-transcendence is one of the strongest elements in the spiritual medicine chest. It is of tremendous therapeutic value because it can provide a cure when you feel most defeated.

Alcoholics Anonymous long ago found that the best person to help an alcoholic is a recovered alcoholic. Logotherapists have found that the best person to help someone in crisis is another person who is struggling with the same crisis and has discovered meaning in spite of it. Widows can help other widows, people in wheelchairs can help others with similar disabilities, the incurably sick can help others who are terminally ill. In helping another, the helping person achieves self-transcendence that leads to meaning (see Chapter Nine).

Self-Distancing

This is the ability to step away from yourself and look at yourself "from the outside." In self-distancing, the spiritual "you" steps away from the physical "you," and often this is the first step necessary for a cure. As long as you say "I am a failure," it will be difficult for you to change, because you consider failure an integral part of yourself. If you learn to say "I am a human being with all sorts of potentials but I have failed in the past," then failure no longer is a part of you but something that you have experienced and that you need not experience again. Physical illness and emotions such as fear and anger are part of your body and psyche, and you can take a stand against them in your spirit. You have, as Frankl expresses it, "the defiant power of the human spirit," a vital resource of your inner medicine chest.

Humor

Thirty years ago Viktor Frankl stressed the importance of humor in medicine. Recently Norman Cousins rediscovered it. Humor is a practical way of self-distancing, of seeing how funny your behavior sometimes seems. The helper does not laugh about you but helps you laugh about yourself. The search for meaning is serious business, but it can be greatly facilitated by humor.

How To Become a Yes-Sayer

Life is difficult. It has more moments of boredom and anguish than moments of joy. Yet if you are aware that life has meaning and offers you a meaning potential in every situation, you will become a yes-sayer regardless of what happens to you.

You have to learn to distinguish two contrasting circumstances: those of fate—which you cannot change—and those of freedom—which you can change. Obviously the meaning in situations you can change lies in the freedom to change them.

It is less obvious to most people that the meaning in an unchangeable situation also lies in freedom—not in the freedom to change what cannot be changed, but in the freedom to change your attitude toward the unavoidable. You can find a meaningful attitude toward something that is meaningless. The negative is not ignored but is guided into positive channels (see Chapter Four).

It is not always easy to distinguish between a situation that can be changed and one that cannot. Death, loss of a limb, restrictions of old age, incurable disease, divorce—these must be accepted or the struggle to change the unchangeable will only weaken you. But in many personal, family, and job situations it is not clear whether meaning lies in fighting the problems or in accepting them. A Socratic dialogue (Chapter Two) can help you make your choice.

The search for meaning is vital for everyone:

- for the young who have not yet found meaning
- for those who had meaning and lost it (midlife crisis)
- for those facing retirement, old age, illness, and death
- for those whose meaning possibilities have changed because of drastically changed life situations, such as loss of a limb, a partner, a career
- for those grieving about a loss experienced because of death, divorce, firing, retirement, accident, sickness
- for those recovering from an addiction
- for those suffering from depression and neurosis
- for those who are bored by their affluence (a relatively new group)

The methods of logotherapy described in this book can help you use the resources of your healthy core, the human spirit. Sometimes this healthy core is blocked by physical illness, psychological disturbance, or addiction. In those cases, other methods—medication, tradition psychotherapy, detoxification—must be used to clear access to the spirit before logotherapy can be applied. This book is for the individual whose healthy core is accessible, whose search for meaning can lead to a fulfilled life.

We are not dealing here with "patients" who are ill. Nor are we dealing with "clients"—that phrase indicates dependency on a professional. We are dealing here with two human beings: a seeker and a helper. The helper may be a professional who uses professional skill to restore health on the physical or psychological level. In the dimension of the spirit, both the seeker and the helper are primarily human beings on the way to finding meaning and becoming yes-sayers to life.

The next three chapters discuss some methods of logotherapy: the Socratic dialogue, dereflection, and modification of attitudes. Chapters Five through Nine give attention to five areas in which meaning is most likely to be found and toward which the search for meaning needs to be directed: self-discovery, choice, uniqueness, responsibility, and self-transcendence. Chapter Ten stresses the usefulness and limitations of values. Chapters Eleven and Twelve contain guidelines for two specific situations: for marriage and family problems, and for groups. The appendixes contain several specific methods developed by logotherapists.

Chapter Two

Socratic Dialogue

The Socratic dialogue is the tool that the helper uses most frequently to aid the seeker in the search for meaning. This dialogue brings you in touch with your healthy core, the spirit, so that you can use its resources.

One of the basic assumptions of logotherapy is that, in the depth of your spiritual dimension, you know what kind of person you are, what your potentials are, what is important and meaningful to you. Socrates believed that it was the task of the teacher, not to pour information into the students, but rather to elicit from the students what they know intuitively. Frankl believes it is the task of the logotherapist, not to tell seekers what the meanings in their lives are, but rather to elicit the wisdom that is hidden within the spirit of each seeker.

Relaxation

The Socratic dialogue helps you achieve access to your spiritual resources. It is wise to get into the right mood before starting a dialogue. If you are excited, nervous, fearful, or despondent, the dialogue should be preceded by a brief relaxation exercise. Many of these exercises are described in detail in *The Relaxation and Stress Reduction Workbook* (Davis, Eshelman, and McKay, 1982). As preparation for a Socratic dialogue, a short exercise of five to ten minutes is usually sufficient:

> The seeker sits in a comfortable position in a chair, with feet planted on the ground, hands on lap, palms open. The helper talks in a low, calming voice; sometimes a short piece of music is played. Three approaches—visual, auditory, and kinesthetic (body sensation)—are available to clear the seeker's path to the unconscious. Some

people react best to one of these approaches, but a combination of the three is usually most effective.

The helper conjures up images of pleasant surroundings—a quiet forest, a sunset on a beach, a flower-filled meadow (for the visual seeker); song birds, bubbling brooks, beautiful music (for the auditory person); and the feeling of being grounded in the earth, relaxing muscles, imagining pleasant warmth or heaviness of the body (for the kinesthetically inclined seeker).

The purpose of this brief exercise is to quiet the chattering of your mind and to find the calm center in yourself. Reading a poem that stresses the positive aspects of life can also be part of this relaxing exercise.

First Questions

The Socratic dialogue uses the five guideposts to probe the areas in which meaning is most likely to be found:

1. Self-discovery. The more you find out about your real self behind all the masks you put on for self protection, the more meaning you will discover.

2. Choice. The more choices you see in your situation, the more meaning will become available.

3. Uniqueness. You are most likely to find meaning in situations where you are not easily replaced by someone else.

4. Responsibility. Your life will be meaningful if you learn to take responsibility where you have freedom of choice, and if you learn not to feel responsible where you face an unalterable fate.

5. Self-transcendence. Meaning comes to you when you reach beyond your egocentricity toward others.

These guideposts, which are discussed more fully in chapters Five to Nine, can be explored by a Socratic dialogue. You start with questions that deal with the situation the seeker is in, and gradually lead to where the seeker wants to be. If you are confronted with a work-related problem, the first question could be: "How do you earn your living?" Follow-up questions could include:

- Where do you see meaning in your work? In the work itself? The people you come in contact with? The product or service your company provides? The prestige it gives you? The money you make?
- What do you do with the money you earn? If you were financially independent, would you want to do the same work you do now?
- What other activities do you have? Hobbies? Volunteer work?
- How many of your activities do you share with your family?
- Would you like to have more time with your family?
- How much time do you spend with your family? With friends?

- Make a "pie chart" that shows how you spend your time.
- Are you satisfied with this distribution?
- In what way would you want to change it? What would you do first to change the distribution of time, to make it fulfill your preference?

Here are some questions that can be used to initiate a Socratic dialogue, and some follow-up questions:

- Under what circumstances do you feel good? If you have difficulty describing such circumstances, make a list of the things that you like to do and mark those you actually have done within the past two weeks.
- What *would* make you feel good?
- What could you do to create a situation in which you would feel good?
- What does "feeling good" mean to you?
- What prevents you from doing things that would make you feel good? How can you overcome those obstacles?
- You feel that you are in a mess now. Tell me about other times when you were in a mess.
- Looking back now, has anything positive come from those situations? Have you learned something from those? Grown? Had experiences you otherwise would not have had?
- Did you risk anything to get out of the mess?
- How did you get out of it?
- Is there anything you can learn from this past experience that can be applied to the current situation?
- What are a few of the things you want to accomplish during the next year? The next three years?
- What keeps you from realizing these things?
- Pick out the one thing you want most to accomplish.
- What would be the first step toward this goal?
- What price would you be willing to pay to achieve this goal?
- Describe situations when you have had the feeling that the world is good and orderly, and you are part of it.
- Is there a quality that is common to these situations?
- How could you achieve this quality now, perhaps in a completely different form?
- Who are your role models?
- What do you admire about them? Do you have any qualities they have?
- Could you achieve some of the qualities you admire in your models?
- What could you do to achieve these qualities, even in a small way?

- Does thinking about these qualities give you an inkling about what kind of person you are? About what kind of person you could be?
- What are your strong points? Your talents?
- What do you need to do to realize your talents?
- What are the obstacles to realizing them? How could you overcome these obstacles?

In logotherapy, the goal is to help the seekers feel good by finding something that is *meaningful* to them, not just something that provides pleasure, money, or power. Remember Frankl's assumption that pleasure is a by-product of having done something meaningful, and that money and power are merely means to an end, not final goals. What meaningful things would the seeker do with money or power?

The Socratic dialogue is not an intellectual discussion, not argumentation or manipulation. Rather, it is teaching/learning that uses experiences—those of the seeker and those of the helper. During the dialogue, the helper elicits ideas and feelings from the seeker by asking questions based on what the seeker says—from "logohints" that the helper finds in the seeker's words.

Picking up Logohints

In a Socratic dialogue the helper does more than listen sympathetically, more than express understanding of the seeker's problems. A mere expression of understanding (a mirroring) of what the seeker is complaining about can enmesh the seeker in the problems even more deeply.

If a seeker says, "I no longer enjoy my life," a helper who is using the principles of logotherapy will *not* say, "I understand that very well after all you have gone through" (expressing understanding) or "You mean you don't want to go on living?" (mirroring). Instead, the response will be, "What about all the tasks out there in life that are still waiting for you?"

In logotherapy, the helper plays a more active role than in most other therapies. The helper listens carefully and picks up phrases that express positive aspects of the seeker. But the helper must be careful not to err by taking too active a part, by trying to persuade.

Persuasion will be effective only when it is based on something the seeker has said that suggests a positive direction. The helper's response needs to pick up on the "logohint"—something positive that the seeker has said—and to suggest some positive attitude or action.

A logohint is a phrase, even a word or a nonverbal indication such as a sudden tone of excitement, that hints at what is meaningful to the seeker, or at a value that is held in high esteem and is manifested in a religious belief, a marital vow, a vocation, or a hobby. These preferences of meaning and values often are stored on an unconscious level, and the helper must have a fine ear to hear these hints from the seeker's unconscious. Logo-hints give the helper the right to support the meaning direction that has been indicated.

Case History

In the Socratic dialogue below, between Ann and a helper, you can see how the helper picked up logohints from what Ann said, and how the helper used the logohints to help Ann help herself.

Ann was a 55-year-old woman who was suffering from depression and headaches. She was divorced, but her three children were successful in their own lives, she lived in a beautiful home, she had no financial worries, and her health had been good until the onset of the depression about a year earlier. Helper:

> *Helper:* Was there a time when you felt really good about yourself?
> *Ann:* I'd say when I was in college.
> *Helper:* What was it about your life then that felt good?
> *Ann:* I wanted to be a dancer. I saw myself on the stage.
> *Helper:* What happened?
> *Ann:* I fell in love with Henry. We got married. I had one child after the other. Oh, I don't regret it. I was busy bringing up the children. I had a good life. Henry was very successful, we entertained, traveled. But now ...
> *Helper:* What has changed?
> *Ann:* We are divorced. The children are gone, one in Massachusetts, one in Florida, one in Australia. I have four grandchildren but I hardly ever see them. Now I'm 55 and alone. No one needs me.

During this fragment of the dialogue, the helper found a logohint: Ann had indicated that the idea of becoming a dancer had been meaningful to her.

> *Helper:* Do you still love dancing?
> *Ann:* Oh yes, I do. I go to the ballet often. But that only makes me sad. I imagine how it would be if *I* were up there on the stage.
> *Helper:* Tell me what you feel.
> *Ann:* Envy. Those girls are young, they are talented, they have careers ahead of them. I think I was as talented as many of them. Perhaps more so. I'll never know.
> *Helper:* Isn't there a way in which you could use your love for dancing, even now?
> *Ann:* Are you kidding? At my age? No, no, life has passed me by.
> *Helper:* Some things have passed. You cannot go back to college and be 18 again. You cannot bring your husband back. You cannot make your children small enough so that they need you. But you can use your love for dancing in a meaningful way, even at 55.

Here the helper is making clear to Ann the difference between the areas of "fate," which she has to accept, and the areas of "freedom," in which she still has choices.

> *Ann:* No, I can't. I tried to get my daughters interested in dancing when they were small, and my grandchildren. But no luck.

Two logohints have now surfaced in the dialogue — Ann's interest in dancing, and her interest in helping children to become dancers. These make it possible for the helper to lead Ann to new meaningful alternatives.

New Alternatives

When seeking new alternatives suggested by logohints, you consider the five guideposts to personal meaning discussed at the beginning of this chapter. Usually it is most practical to start with the area of choice.

The seeker is guided to convert the logohints into a series of alternatives, and to examine the positive and negative consequences of each alternative. The method for doing this is described in detail in Chapter Six. The seeker is encouraged to include as many alternatives as possible, even those that may seem impractical. This is done to show the seeker that he or she is not trapped, that choices are available.

Next, the seeker decides which alternative is best. "Best" is understood to mean, not necessarily the most pleasant, remunerative, or prestigious (although pleasure, money, or prestige may be a by-product), but the most meaningful in the situation at hand. All five areas of meaning are considered. Choice, of course, has center stage, but the other five areas are also important. Among the questions that deal with choice are the following:

- Does your final choice from among the alternatives express your personality (self-discovery), rather than an "ought" that comes from outside yourself?
- Does your choice express your uniqueness? Does it create a situation in which you are, at least to some extent, irreplaceable?
- Does your choice consider the interests of other people (responsibility)? Is it harmful to others or to your relationship with others?
- Is your choice helpful to others who are important to you, or to a cause you want to support (self-transcendence)? This does not mean that you must not have any selfish motivations. It does mean, however, that you extend your interest beyond yourself to include other people and causes. You will find that fulfillment is a by-product of helping others.

After choosing the best alternative, the seeker takes concrete steps to implement that alternative. The decision must be translated into action.

Application of Alternative

During the Socratic dialogue, Ann made lists as she sought guideposts to meaning. She was encouraged to make a list of alternatives that included her love for dancing and for children. At this point she raised —as many people do —a number of "yes, but" objections: Yes, but —she was no longer young; she did not keep up with modern dancing trends; she had no talent for organizing, no business sense; she didn't know any talented children. The helper encouraged Ann to list all the alternatives she could think of, and to list her "yes, but" arguments as negative consequences. The helper must be careful, at this stage of the dialogue, not to "prescribe" alternative solutions, but instead to "describe" a number of alternatives and let the seeker decide which to include in the list.

After considerable prodding, Ann made a list that included the following:

- Volunteer to work in a dancing school for children. ("What could I do there? Answer the phone? Keep records? Any high school girl could do that.")
- Help the dance instructors with ideas about teaching dance. ("My ideas are out of date. They would laugh at me.")
- Go to classes to learn about modern trends in dance. ("I am too old to go to school.")
- Establish a dance school. ("I'm not a business woman. I would fail.")
- Buy an established dance school. ("I do not have enough money for that.")
- Help dance school graduates obtain engagements. ("I have no talent for that.")
- Find a talented girl who cannot afford dance school, and help her with her career. ("How can I find such a girl?")

When Ann looked over her list, she showed some interest in the last alternative. Then the helper was justified in supporting this choice by following it up in a Socratic dialogue.

Helper: Doing that would not require much money and it would give you personal contact with a young woman who is beginning to dance, as you once were.

Ann: (tentatively) I could give that girl the chance I gave up.

Helper: It would make a crucial difference in that girl's life.

Ann: (warming up to the idea) I could spare her the disappointments I had. I could go to some of the classes with her. I could give her some advice. I think I do still do know something about dancing that could be valuable. Yes, I'd like to try that.

Helper: What would be the first step you would take?

At this point in the dialogue, the helper and the seeker are going through the important transition from self-chosen goal to action. With some suggestions from the helper, Ann made a list of ways to find the girl she would help: Put an ad in the newspapers. Go to a welfare agency and make inquiries. Go to dance schools. Then, abruptly, Ann crumpled up the list.

> *Ann:* No, I want to find her myself.
> *Helper:* How would you do that?
> *Ann:* I have a good eye for kids who have talent. I would go through poor neighborhoods and watch children at play.

Ann searched for a child and found an adopted Korean girl. And Ann helped that girl to start a career as a dancer.

Ann's decision encompassed all five guideposts to meaning:

- She discovered what she really wanted at this particular stage in her life, rather than what her friends approved of, or what her counselor suggested.
- She saw that she had choices, that she was not trapped in a stage of life that seemed empty.
- She felt that she could do something in which she would feel irreplaceable.
- The choice considered other people, and her financial limitations.
- Most important, the choice clearly was self-transcending—she helped another human being and felt fulfilled.

Techniques of the Dialogue

Like other logotherapeutic techniques, the Socratic dialogue requires a lot of improvisation and intuition. There are many ways to probe a person's unconscious and its hidden knowledge about personal meanings. The Socratic dialogue uses certain methods. Among these are:

- recall of past meaningful experiences;
- dream interpretations that focus on unconscious hopes and wishes rather than on repressed traumas;
- guided and unguided fantasies to reveal what the seeker considers meaningful;
- meaningful experiences of people the seeker considers to be role models; and
- recall of peak experiences that have shown the seeker, often in a flash, that life does have meaning.

Recalling Experiences

The experiences of both the seeker and the helper are used in the search for meaning. If you ask a person who feels negative, "When did your life have meaning?" you are not likely to receive a positive answer. A preferred approach is to ask, "When was there a time when you felt happy or good about yourself?" This question encourages the seeker to reminisce about the past, looking for experiences that were positive, rather than for abstract positive meanings.

Here is part of a dialogue between a helper and a seeker, Harry, who was living in self-chosen isolation. Harry talked about his life. Eventually he said:

> *Harry:* I never married after I saw what my mother did to my father. He became an alcoholic, beat me up. I was a poor student in school, and the kids all teased me because I was no good in sports. If it hadn't been for Tom, I don't know how I'd have survived.
>
> *Helper:* Tell me about Tom.
>
> *Harry:* Tom was a neighbor, two years older. We collected stamps together, and went hiking in wilderness areas. We did a lot of things together. And he was always supportive when things were bad at home with my parents.

Gradually Harry became less negative. He remembered other people who were supportive. He began to move away from being a no-sayer, in spite of his conviction that "most people are beasts."

In later dialogues Harry recalled situations in which some people "were a little less beastly than the rest of the human zoo" (his form of humor). He decided to join a hiking club and a stamp club. The helper recognized Harry's earlier mentions of engaging in these activities with Tom as logohints and so felt justified in supporting these choices. And the helper suggested to Harry that he make an orderly collection from the odd boxes of stamps in his basement (a task to fulfill), and that he help a boy in his neighborhood to start a stamp collection (self-transcendence). These actions were small first steps on Harry's way back to the human community.

The use of past experiences as the basis for future activities is especially helpful for people who feel negative, empty, depressed, and alienated, and for people who are bored because of their affluence.

Dreams

Sigmund Freud called dreams the royal road to the unconscious. Viktor Frankl agrees, and sees the unconscious not only in a psychological but also in a spiritual dimension as a royal road into a much wider land. It can lead to meaning.

The unconscious that Freud described contains repressed thoughts and feelings that we don't want to face consciously. Repression can cause neurosis curable by psychoanalysis. Frankl has an expanded concept of the unconscious. He asserts that it contains, also, repressed hopes, goals, and meanings to which dreams are "royal roads." Repressed meanings do not necessarily cause neurosis, but an inner emptiness into which neurosis can enter, especially in conflicts of conscience or existential frustration. For these disturbances, logotherapy is indicated.

Dreams may make you aware of repressed drives and traumas that are too painful to face. But dreams may also contain and convey advice from the conscience. A dream interpretation from this perspective can help you discover what is meaningful.

Case History

Betty, a 34-year-old woman who did not get along with her father, dreamed that she lay in bed with him and embraced him tenderly, and he responded. Alarmed, she awoke. Was it possible that she had repressed incestuous desires, after all the rejections she had experienced since childhood? Her father had always preferred her older brother, had never spent much time with her, was never satisfied with her grades although she was a good student, was very strict with her, and so on.

A logotherapeutic dream interpretation revealed a different explanation. Perhaps the dream was saying: "Be nice to your father, and he will be nice to you." The young woman phoned her father (he lived two hundred miles away) and asked him whether she could visit—something she almost never did.

"What do you want?" he growled.

Under ordinary circumstances that question would have been enough to irritate her. This time she simply said she wanted to have dinner with him. She went to see him and, still under the impact of her dream, she responded to his mistrust with gentleness. After that she visited her father every two weeks, and talked with him about the years of her childhood. Her brother had been born with a clubfoot and needed more attention. She was healthy and gifted; her father was proud of her and had prodded her to get even better grades. He wanted her to go to college, to become a doctor or a lawyer. The young woman began to see her childhood in a new light. A few weeks before her father died, a year later, he told her: "I'm glad that I got to know you as one adult to another." The logotherapeutic interpretation of her dream had given them the opportunity to do that.

Frankl published several case histories in which the dream was the royal road to the conscience. Tony, a composer who wrote cheap music for the movies, dreamed he wanted to make a telephone call but the dial on the phone was so complicated that he couldn't select the right number. He wanted to dial the number of a woman for whom, during a recent summer, he had composed religious music that had given him great artistic satisfaction. He had no romantic intentions—their relationship was purely professional. The dream did not reveal repressed sexual desires; it represented the voice of his conscience, which seemed to be telling him: "Choose between composing cheap music for a lot of money and composing music that really satisfies you, even if the income is less." No wonder that dialing (choosing) had been difficult. In German, the same word—wählen—means choosing and dialing.

A logotherapeutic interpretation of a dream can reveal the deepest reason for a depression or a neurosis, the spiritual causes for physical or psychosomatic illnesses, the direction that you really want to go in a conflict situation. Dreams can also give advice, from your unconscious to your conscious self. Frankl reports a case of a mother who dreamed that she put her favorite cat in the washing machine. When she opened the machine to hang up the wash, the cat was dead. When this woman engaged in a Socratic dialogue, she discovered this interpretation: Her favorite cat represented her favorite daughter, Joan. The mother disapproved of Joan's lifestyle, and she often criticized Joan, even in front of other people. The dream was a warning: "Don't wash 'dirty linen' in public, or you may lose your daughter!"

Dreams have many functions in logotherapy. They can be useful for starting a Socratic dialogue, or for getting one off dead center. A widow had withdrawn from her circle of friends. In a dream she saw a college professor she had greatly admired. But she was disappointed when he quoted an overused piece of Greek wisdom: "The unexamined life is not worth living." Not until the next day did she realize that in her dream the professor had reversed the idea, saying to her "The unlived life is not worth examining." You could say that Socrates himself helped this widow as she went on from that realization through a Socratic dialogue to find direction.

Unguided Fantasies

Dreams have two disadvantages. First, you cannot create a dream at will. And second, dreams speak in a hard-to-understand, symbolic language. Fantasies, both unguided and guided, can be more directly helpful.

To elicit fantasies, the seeker must be in a quiet mood that has stopped the "chattering of the mind," so that images can float up freely from the unconscious. Any kind of meditation—or a few minutes from a relaxation tape, or a poem read in a calm voice—can be used to achieve a quiet state.

An unguided fantasy can be the starting point of a Socratic dialogue — for those who see no meaning in life, no goal or purpose, no task, nothing worth striving for. They may be the young who have not yet discovered meaningful direction in their lives, or those in midlife crises, or people whose meaning possibilities have changed because the circumstances of their lives have changed. The helper can elicit such a fantasy by asking the seeker to imagine that one year has passed (or three, or five) then giving no other instructions except saying something like: "It's Monday morning and you wake up. Describe where you are and what you do."

As the seeker replies, prompted as necessary by questions from the helper, logohints turn up. One young man saw himself married, with a child, working in a hospital as a male nurse. The Socratic dialogue could then be pointed in a particular direction: How could this young man combine his wish for a family with the training he would need to become a nurse? He was earning a fair amount of money as a salesman, a job he hated and wanted to give up. And he was spending much of his earnings at bars and race tracks. Was he willing to keep his unwanted job as a salesman so that he could save money to use to go back to college and eventually take on the responsibility of having a family? The young man decided that this long-range goal was worth the temporary sacrifices.

A dramatic example of a Socratic dialogue based on unguided fantasy was provided by a high school girl. She had wanted to become a librarian, but then had lost her eyesight as the result of an accident with a rifle. A therapist helped this young woman through the process of grieving for her lost sight. But she was still in deep despair about her future. In an unguided fantasy, she saw herself as a librarian. A blind man came to her and asked her to read to him. She told him that she was blind herself.

The young woman discussed various possibilities with the helper, who worked with logohints found in the unguided fantasy: The young woman wanted to help other blind people, and she still wanted to be a librarian. The helper suggested several scenarios in which these two goals could be combined. The blind girl decided to become a librarian in a school for the blind. With this self-transcending task challenging her, the young woman overcame her depression, finished high school, learned Braille, and went to library school.

Ann, the middle-aged woman who decided to help a young, aspiring dancer, used unguided fantasy to think through how she would accomplish that goal. She talked about seeing herself wandering through playgrounds, talking to girls, making friends with their mothers, inviting them to her home, testing their talent, selecting one special girl, contacting the right school, and guiding the girl—with financial and human support—through her career until she stood on the stage for the first time.

Guided Fantasies

When a Socratic dialogue meanders and comes to a halt, guided fantasy can be used. It is facilitated with symbols and images. The individual thinks about a particular kind of setting, then begins to define that in specific terms.

A forest can represent the way you see your life. Dark, threatening, confusing, or lush and fragrant, with hills and flowers. No path, or a clear path, a lot of forks in the road, a lot of undergrowth. Roots to stumble over, or berries to pick.

A mountain can represent striving, hopes. Steep, no path, rugged, frightening. Inviting, with broad rocks, rocks that encourage climbing.

A creek or stream can represent the course of life. You can follow it to your source—your past—or to its mouth—your future. You can swim in it, row on it, wander alongside it, sit on the shore and watch, fish. It can be full of rapids. It can have natural or man-made dams. It can flow peacefully, rush gently, be refreshing, inviting, threatening. It can meander through a meadow full of flowers or through a dark forest, over boulders, into a plain or desert or swamp.

A building—can represent your person. A simple farm house or a palace, a large apartment building, a ramshackle hut, a suburban villa, built by yourself or designed by an architect. With a vegetable or herb or flower garden, well groomed or wild. With a swimming pool, backyard, play area. In a slum, downtown, in a suburb or the country. With a basement (the unconscious), few or many rooms (the conscious life), and an attic (the mind), with views—to a beautiful garden or a bare wall.

Many images can be given symbolic meaning: a ship on a high sea, an empty or full granary, dangerous or friendly animals, vehicles (cars, planes, ships, gondolas). You can introduce many people into a guided fantasy— father, mother, partner, child, friend, enemy, boss, stranger.

While unguided fantasy is helpful for people with a general feeling of meaninglessness, guided fantasy is helpful with a specific problem.

Example 1: Lack of self-confidence. The seeker is guided toward a situation that will strengthen self-image. To encourage the seeker to begin the fantasy, the helper makes suggestions:

"You are standing in a meadow full of flowers. It is a sunny day. The sky is blue and birds are singing. You walk slowly through the meadow, on a path toward a building. When you get there, you find that the door is locked. You ring the bell, but no one answers. You want to get into the building. You walk around it, trying other doors. Finally you find one that is open. You go inside and find yourself in a room full of people, all talking in small groups. They are all people you know, some friends, some casual acquaintances. You are aware that they cannot see you. You are surprised that they are all talking about you, and they are all saying positive things. You go from one group to another, listening. What are they saying?"

The images are chosen to fit the needs. In this example, the person who lacks self-confidence is placed in happy surroundings (flowers, birds, sunshine), on a definite path toward a place in life (the building). An effort is needed to find access (the doors are locked), but the effort pays off (one door is open). The rest of the imagery is based on the premise that, deep within, we know our strong points, which have been repressed and need to be made conscious.

The same goal can be achieved through another guided fantasy, one based on the seeker's realization that at a memorial service only the good aspects of the deceased are mentioned:

"Imagine that you are attending your own memorial service. Your favorite music is being played. Your favorite minister (or rabbi or lay friend) gives a eulogy and then asks those present to speak up and tell what they remember about you, and why they are sad that you died."

Example 2: A difficult decision that needs to be made. The answer is buried in your unconscious. You are led through pleasant surroundings and are asked to enter a dark, wide room with a figure dimly visible in the distance.

You approach the figure slowly, wondering who it might be but certain that it is an important figure in your life, a person who will have the answer you are seeking. You think about the question you need to answer as you approach the distant figure. You know that you will be able to ask only one question. Finally you are close enough to recognize the figure. You face the figure and ask your question, and eagerly await the answer. Then the figure speaks. Who was the figure? What was your question? What was the answer?

In this and other fantasies, the guidelines must be nondirective. The helper says "building," not "house" or "villa" or "shack." The word "figure" is used, not "man" or "woman." "He" and "she" are avoided. So is any indication of whether the figure is young or old, a real person or a figure from religious or secular literature. The identification by the seeker provides logohints that can then be used to carry the dialogue forward. Some seekers will see *themselves* as the figure. This indicates that, deep within, they know the answer to the question. Others will see a religious figure or an important person in their lives—perhaps a parent, grandparent, friend, teacher. One man saw the grandfather whom, as a child, he had helped on a farm. This seeker was trying to decide whether to leave his wife. The grandfather said, "You can't plant a peach tree and expect to get cherries." That answer led to a discussion about how much the man could expect his wife to change, and that discussion became the basis the couple used to work out their difficulties.

Another man was in despair because he had lost a leg. What was he to do in this new situation? He saw his favorite teacher, a person he credited with having a great influence on his life. The teacher was wearing a long coat, which he lifted to reveal that he, too, had only one leg. The teacher said nothing, but smiled. This fantasy opened up a Socratic dialogue that led to the realization that handicaps, too, can be great teachers. The helper and the seeker talked about what the seeker, as a man with only one leg, could still do that would be meaningful for him.

Example 3: Conflicting values. The founder and owner of a successful company was suffering from headaches and depressions, and also from some marital problems. The helper suspected a conflict between the man's devotion to his business and the attention he was giving to his wife and children. In a guided fantasy, the man was led into a dark cellar (his unconscious). When his eyes got used to the darkness, the man saw that the room was filled with packages, small and large, some wrapped gaily and others in newspapers or cartons. He was allowed to poke and shake the packages, to guess what was in them, but he was not allowed to open them. After he had explored for a while, the man was told to pick the one package that he wanted. And then he was allowed to take the chosen package to the lighted room upstairs and open it. He was disappointed to find that it contained a bust of Richard Wagner. That made no sense to him, because he didn't care for music and especially not for Wagner. He was then told to go downstairs again and select a second package, and bring it upstairs. Again he was disappointed—the second package contained a Monopoly game, something he had not played since his children were small and that he had always considered a waste of time. The man was allowed to go to the cellar a third time to pick a third package, with the understanding that this would be his last chance. When he unwrapped it in the light, he was disappointed once more. The third package contained a plastic Christmas tree and cheap but colorful decorations. Christmas had little meaning for him, and he had always resented spending money on decorations that were used only once a year, or even thrown away.

In the Socratic dialogue that followed, this man had an "aha" experience. He realized that the message contained in the three packages was: "Play, relax, enjoy! Don't be a workaholic! Music (Wagner), games (Monopoly), celebrations (Christmas trees)." He followed the advice of his unconscious and his depression disappeared.

Experiences of Others

At different times in our lives, we have all had role models. The experiences of such role models can be useful in advancing a Socratic dialogue, especially for the person who has suffered a loss or is caught in some trap from which there seems to be no escape. Many people have been inspired by the stories of Helen Keller and Franklin Roosevelt, who led meaningful lives in spite of their handicaps.

Leland Stanford, the California railroad builder, lost his son just as the boy was about to enter college. Stanford decided to establish a university to enable other young people to get the education his son no longer could get. Recently Stanford's story was told to a woman who had lost her son just as he was about to enter college. She was, of course, not able to start a university. But during a Socratic dialogue she decided to establish a scholarship that would enable at least one student each year to afford a university career. She found some comfort and meaning in administering the fund and selecting recipients.

Viktor Frankl's experiences in the concentration camps have inspired many people to find meaning in their own analogous experiences — situations that were, for them, traps from which they could not escape. In a Socratic dialogue, one must be careful not to deprecate the seeker's problems. However, many people, as they have discussed their situations in Socratic dialogues, have come to the conclusion that "if Frankl could survive the death camps and build a meaningful life, I can find meaning in my life." One woman, whose husband left her at about the same time she lost her job, read Frankl's book, *Man's Search for Meaning*. Afterward she said "Frankl made me aware that my spiritual pilot light was still on." A Socratic dialogue can turn up that spiritual pilot light and get life bubbling again.

Peak Experiences

A peak experience can spark a Socratic dialogue. The helper cannot bring about a peak experience during a dialogue. But certainly the helper can point out the meaning-carrying messages of such an experience when it is recalled by the seeker during a Socratic dialogue.

The helper must keep a keen ear open for such episodes, which the seeker may mention only in passing, and without recognizing the value of such memories in the search for meaning. Many peak experiences are incidents that are hardly noticed when they occur, but which are nevertheless effective in keeping the spiritual pilot light burning.

Peak experiences often occur in painful situations. A man recounted an incident he had carried as if it were a burden and had not spoken of in three years. His wife had died after a long siege of cancer. The day after her funeral, he had had to take a plane trip. During the flight, the plane broke through the clouds and reached bright sunlight. Looking out the window of the plane as the sunlight filled the sky, the widower felt a sudden burst of joy, and then immediately felt guilty for having experienced that moment of joy. Three years later, when he was going through a period of depression, the widower told a friend about that experience, citing it as proof that there was "something wrong" with him. His friend replied that, on the contrary, life might have wanted in the memorable moment to provide him with proof that "something was right" with him, to show him that the sun shines, even behind the clouds.

Another man told of an incident that occurred as he was driving down a lonely road, feeling alienated. Suddenly a fox started to cross the road and then stopped in the middle. The man stepped on the brakes, the car came to a halt ten feet from the animal, and the man and the fox looked at each other. Recounting this incident, the man recalled that at that moment he had felt in harmony with all of nature, with the whole universe.

A woman who had been blind for two years had an operation that was to restore her sight. When her eyes had healed, the bandages were taken off. Recalling that moment, the woman described the exhilaration she felt when she looked down, as the last bandage was removed, and for the first time in two years was able to see the grain in the wood of the floor.

It is extremely difficult to convince a person by intellectual arguments that life has meaning under all circumstances, that we are each part of a totality and not alone, or that there are affirmative aspects in situations of pain. The seeker who recalls such peak experiences may find unexpected and helpful insights.

A Socratic dialogue can draw attention to such incidents, which are often disregarded when they occur or are soon forgotten. The messages of such experiences, though they are buried in the spirit, need to be heard. Those messages can be evoked during a Socratic dialogue and can help the seeker turn toward positive attitudes.

Playback of the Positive

The Socratic dialogue probes the unconscious spirit. It is in the spirit that you keep your repressed or ignored will to meaning, your hopes and dreams, your buried goals, your neglected self-esteem, and many positive aspects of yourself that unhappy or misunderstood experiences in your past have repressed. During the Socratic dialogue, bits of these dreams, goals, and experiences emerge. It is up to the helper to pick up those pieces and "play them back" to the seeker.

Case History

James Yoder is a logotherapist in Kansas City. Yoder tells about Fred, a gifted professional who was struggling with self-deprecating attitudes, guilt, and the problems of a no-sayer. Here is a segment of their dialogue, in which Yoder picked up affirmative phrases that had emerged from Fred's unconscious and then played those phrases back to Fred so that he became conscious of them:

Fred: (after telling about his life, which he described as full of failures and disappointments): I'm afraid sometimes to take another step—not sure whether it will make sense.

Yoder: Let's look at your past. If your past is like a web a spider spins (Fred had used that phrase), what kind of web do you spin? Your life seems to contain jewels of achievements, experiences, relationships.

Fred: (weeping): Yes, I would say so.

Yoder: No one can take them away from you. What do you learn from looking at your past, full of such jewels?

Fred: I do learn, even though I really feel down and deserted. A part of me is resting up, getting ready to take another shot at life, later.

Fred tells Yoder that he read Frankl's account of his experiences in the concentration camps.

> *Fred:* I've been thinking about Frankl all week, ever since I read that.
>
> *Yoder:* What goes through your mind?
>
> *Fred:* I must say, pessimism. I see myself as probably being one of those who would not have survived, emotionally, spiritually, and yet that's not entirely true. I have some hope for myself. I see myself as one of the 99 percent who did not remain spiritually intact . . . as one who would sell my brothers to stay alive . . . but the fact that Frankl shows that some did not compromise and they still stayed alive proves that one can survive.
>
> *Yoder:* Talk about hope. I heard you say you still have hope.
>
> *Fred:* Yes, I . . . I refuse to write myself off. And yet . . . Fred slides back into stories about rejections and traps.
>
> *Yoder:* As Frankl says, every person has his or her own concentration camp. Tell me about yours, and about your emergence, your hope. The very fact that you sit here today discussing your pain, your freedom of choice . . . your mention of hope demonstrates that you have survived.
>
> *Fred:* (sighs and smiles): Well . . . I think that's true. How did I manage to get out? Certain people cared about me.

Fred then told about a high school teacher who took a personal interest in him, a bishop who treated him tenderly and accepted him when Fred's father brought him to the church and presented him to the bishop as a liar.

> *Yoder:* Instead of criticism and judgment, you experienced acceptance.
>
> *Fred:* (weeping) Yes. Oddly enough, some colleagues seem to like me. It warms my heart.
>
> *Yoder:* What do you believe they like about you?
>
> *Fred:* That I am gentle, that I have an infectious smile. That I have a light touch, a sense of humor. That there is a simplicity or innocence about me, sometimes. I'm not the one who devours.
>
> *Yoder:* You tell me what you are not—"I'm not the one who devours." Tell me the positive about yourself.
>
> *Fred:* I am a person who is sensitive to other people's needs.
>
> *Yoder:* Such people have friends.
>
> *Fred:* I don't feel as if I have any friends . . . I fear getting support and help from others. I'm afraid I'll be told "you want too much."
>
> *Yoder:* In spite of the negative feelings you have shared with me, there were people who listened to you, who were gentle with you and shared your pain.

During another session, Fred told about a dream in which he wanted to use an electric saw.

Fred: I looked at my own "power package" (puts his hand on his chest). It was all rusted and corroded inside. I was afraid to put my hand on it for fear I would be electrocuted.

Yoder: You have talked about people who care about you, and about accomplishments you are proud of. In spite of this dream, and even though you say the machinery is old, that your "power plant is rusty," somehow you have energy flowing through you out to others, and you rise above your pain and past neglect.

Fred: (weeping) A silver wire reaches from my center out into the green woods. But I fear that I am the destroyer . . . I fear I will be the shark.

Yoder: Maybe the very fact that you say you fear, that you will become the devouring shark, points out how very much you value treating others with gentleness and respect. Your fear even enlightens the value of the silver wire, showing you how you want to live your life.

Fred: Yes. Yes. I didn't see that so clearly before.

This was the turning point of the session. Fred had become receptive to seeing himself in a more positive light. Yoder commented on this dialogue: "Always the clients are affirmed for their positive and courageous stands amidst all their suffering. From this session alone, I knew that Fred was well along the road to recovery, transcending his feeling of meaningless and depression.

The Buried Decision

The helper in a Socratic dialogue has to really listen, so that each logohint—even if it is buried in a flood of seemingly irrelevant statements—is heard and used.

Case History

Here is part of a dialogue between Margaret and her helper. Margaret arrived for the session in an agitated state, disturbed because the woman with whom she was sharing an apartment had given Margaret notice that she was to move out.

Margaret: I've moved three times this past year. It's so hard to find a place where I feel happy. Now I've finally found a place, but Ann doesn't like me. And she has the lease. I'm trapped.

Helper: What makes you think she doesn't like you?

Margaret: Nothing I do suits her.

Helper: Be specific. [General statements should be challenged.]

Margaret: She says I leave the kitchen in a mess. She doesn't like me to smoke. She says Blackie [Margaret's cat] scratches up her furniture. I play my stereo too loud for her. And she doesn't want me to use the kitchen when her boyfriend is there.

Helper: Do those things mean that she doesn't like *you*?

Margaret: I know she doesn't. I clean up the kitchen, even her mess, I go outside to smoke, but no matter what I do, she finds something wrong. She knows I love this house more than anything but she wants me out. I have no choice.

Helper: You have already made your choice.

Margaret: (startled) Huh?

Helper: Listen to what you said: "It's hard to find a place where I feel happy... Now I've finally found a place ... I love this house more than anything ..."

Margaret: That's true but now I have to leave.

Helper: No, you just have to pay a price to stay.

Margaret: It's not a matter of money.

Helper: I don't mean money. You told me in our first session that you ran away with a boyfriend to get out of your parents' home. Then you left your boyfriend because he became rough when he drank. Then you moved from one place to another because you didn't like each one. You didn't make all these moves because you had no choice. It was your choice, each time.

Margaret: And now I'm trapped.

Helper: You're trapped in your own behavior pattern. But you do have a choice. To change this pattern or to go on with it.

Margaret: Of course I don't want to spend my life moving. What can I do?

The helper had the right to suggest a solution because she had heard Margaret say, without realizing that she was saying it, that she wanted to stay in this house—that she was ready to pay the price, ready to change her pattern. Under the guidance of the helper, Margaret made a list of things that she could do that might persuade her housemate to let her stay. By the end of the session Margaret had a list of eight alternatives.

"Your price list," the helper said. "Which of these do you choose?"

One of the alternatives was a strict schedule that gave Margaret and her housemate the run of the house every second day. Each one, on her day, had to do the cleaning, but she could also have her boyfriend over on that day. The "contract" for this schedule contained agreements about smoking, noise levels, and other sources of conflict.

"She'll never agree," Margaret said as she left the session.

"Try it," the helper advised. "And when you show this to your housemate, tell her: "I made up these suggestions because I love this house and *you*."

At the next session Margaret reported that her housemate had made a few changes but then had accepted the proposal. They had celebrated their contract by having a party on Sunday with both of their boyfriends, and afterward they had cleaned up the kitchen together.

The Socratic dialogue is often used in connection with two logotherapeutic methods that are discussed in the next two chapters: dereflection, and modification of attitudes.

Chapter Three

Dereflection

Dereflection will help you discover meaning in situations where you feel trapped by your own worry about a problem. The problem may be physical, psychological, or existential—that is, a problem of living in the world as it is. Dereflection will not cure a purely physical problem, such as deafness or arthritis, but it will free you from the additional problem that comes from thinking too much about a problem.

One difficulty in deciding how to get out of an unwanted situation is the tendency to worry. There is no situation that cannot be made worse by excessive worrying. A certain amount of worrying is healthy: it will get you to seek medical or other help. But if you brood on a problem, eventually you will feel as if you are the helpless victim of a problem you cannot solve. It is in situations such as this that dereflection can be applied productively.

Although any problem becomes harder to bear if you think too much about it, it is difficult to decide *not* to think about a problem. The more you want not to think about something, the more you think about it. Remember the story about the man who was promised $100 if he would not think of a chameleon? Although he had never before thought about this strange creature, now suddenly he could not stop thinking about it. But as soon as he was told to think about an elephant, he stopped thinking about the chameleon.

That's the principle behind dereflection. If your problem is caused by too much reflection (what logotherapists call "hyperreflection"), the help comes from *de*reflection.

Hyperreflecting people take themselves too seriously. Not only do they hyperreflect on their problems, they also "hyperintend"—they pay too much attention to solving their problems with will power. And yet often it is hyperintention that makes it impossible to solve a problem. Dereflection strengthens your capacity for self-transcendence—your ability to reach out beyond self-centeredness toward other people or goals that are meaningful to you.

Unhealthy hyperreflection may focus on a **single symptom** such as a sleep disturbance or a sexual dysfunction. Or it may be a **general attitude toward life**. In either of these situations, hyperreflection is an effort to force a change to occur. In both situations, dereflection can be helpful. Dereflection consists of two parts: a *stop sign* that puts the brakes on pathological hyperreflection, and a *guidepost* that turns the mind to other thoughts. This new direction gradually creates a positive, meaning-oriented (rather than ego-centered) view of the world.

Note: If a problem has physical causes, medical and pharmaceutical help must be sought; dereflection may then be used as a complementary strategy. Most difficulties discussed here have psychological origins and can be helped by dereflection. But a medical diagnosis is recommended before a therapy plan is entered.

Single Symptoms

Sleep Disturbance

The more attention you pay to a sleep disturbance, the harder it is to cure. If you lie in bed, awake, worrying about falling asleep, you block the natural mechanism that leads to sleep. This hyperreflection is quickly followed by hyperintention: you *want* to fall asleep, become nervous because you are still awake, and worry about the harmful effects that a sleepless night will have on your activities during the coming day. The more you think about the problem the more it keeps you awake and the less likely you are to fall asleep.

Application: As the stop sign, you are told that the human body manages, under any circumstances, to get the minimum number of hours of sleep that it needs. Instead of worrying about not falling asleep, you are advised to think (using a kind of paradoxical intention): "It's good to be awake. This is a gift of living time. I sleep away a third of my life, anyway."

As the guidepost, you are encouraged to think of other things—for example, to review the day just over, or to make a plan for the coming weekend, or to read all but the last three pages of a short story and then to think about how the story may end.

Sexual Dysfunction

A man who keeps watching himself to see if he gets an erection will hardly feel anything. Nor will a woman who keeps observing her physical responses. Sexual pleasure cannot be forced. If you chase after it, you chase it away. The consequences can include psychogenic impotence, frigidity, and insecurity about sex roles, and these lead to tension during the sexual encounter and fixate the dysfunction.

Application: For this problem, there may be no more effective stop sign than a doctor's order of "no intercourse" for a certain length of time. This removes the demand for sexual performance. Coitus is not expected, and strained self-observation becomes senseless. The client is advised to explain to the sexual partner that the doctor has ordered temporary celibacy for health reasons.

The guidepost in this situation directs the client to be loving, gentle, and attentive with his partner, to help her experience pleasure instead of thinking about his own. This automatically regenerates potency. When the dysfunction has disappeared, the prescription for temporary celibacy is no longer needed or observed.

This change of behavior and attitude is as effective for female nonresponsiveness as for male impotence. When orgasm is not the goal of intercourse, it is more likely to occur.

Other Body Dysfunctions

Similar hyperreflection mechanisms are at work in psychogenic disturbances of activities that require automatic, unreflected body functions, such as speech, movement, and eating. If you pay too much attention to how you form words, or if you are conscious of your tongue and lips, you are in danger of stuttering. Similarly harmful is excessive observation of chewing and swallowing movements in eating, or of body and foot movements while dancing. Only when you forget your feet and automatically follow the music can you stay in rhythm.

Application: Here the stop sign refers not to the activity itself but rather to the hyperintention to do the activity right. You cannot tell people to stop talking, eating, and walking, but you may tell them to stop observing bodily functions that are automatic and best left to the body. Attention is focused on the guideposts: stutterers are advised to pay attention to *what* they say rather than to *how* they say it—to look at the meaning of their words, to what they communicate to their audience. People with psychological eating difficulties are advised to let the gullet do the swallowing and to concentrate on table conversation or on watching a favorite television program. Similarly, nervous dancers are told to pay less attention to their feet and more to their dancing partners and the music.

Elisabeth Lukas, director of the South German Institute of Logotherapy, tells about a little girl who could not learn how to swim because she paid too much attention to her arm and feet movements. The mother bought a tape recording of the girl's favorite fairy tales, and played it while the child was in the water. Within minutes the girl was able to swim while listening to the tape. From that moment on she could swim, even without the help of the tape. Once she had broken the cycle of failure and hyperreflection, she no longer saw herself as the helpless victim of her problem but as the master of the situation.

Dereflection will not work that swiftly in all situations. People who have stuttered or have had eating dysfunctions for a long time will have to practice dereflection for a while before they are able to overcome the difficulty. Often professional help is required.

General Attitudes Toward Life

Sometimes hyperreflection is focused not on a single symptom but on a general negative attitude. The excessive worry may be triggered by some event, usually a failure, or it may have no special trigger. Both triggered and untriggered hyperreflections produce lasting discomfort.

Triggered Hyperreflection

Divorce, loss of a child, break-up of a love relationship, inability to have a child, failure to find a satisfying job—any of these could be a trigger. An example is a man who has finished the training for his profession but cannot find a suitable position. He seems to have no other interests. All he talks about is what it would be like to work in his field. He blames "God and the world" for his situation, and he does nothing to change it.

This man's thinking focuses on his disappointment, and thus he blocks his own flexibility, his ability to respond more reasonably to his situation. This man fixates on his status quo, just as the insomniac fixates on his sleeplessness. The trigger for such hyperreflection need not be a serious blow of fate. Even minor difficulties can provoke pathological consequences.

Application: When hyperreflection is triggered, you must determine whether the trigger belongs in the area of fate or in the area of freedom. Dereflection is applied in the area of freedom.

The man in the above example may be unable to find work because of the situation in the job-market, which is beyond his control and therefore an area of fate. In that situation the technique of modification of attitudes (discussed in Chapter Four) will be helpful.

However, the jobless man also has an area of freedom. The helper directs the man's attention to this area—toward whatever potential he has for free choice. He is encouraged to stop looking for job opportunities in fields that are closed to him, and to look for guideposts to the areas open to him—to seek meaningful activities and solutions in new places. This does not solve his original problem (the need to find work), but it prevents him from engaging in extreme hyperreflection on other failures and from developing a negative attitude toward life.

Untriggered Hyperreflection

Some people constantly hyperreflect on their well-being. Such hyper-reflection actually interferes with well-being. In the morning, they brood about whether they slept well, whether they had bad dreams, whether breakfast was nutritious, whether to go to work. The more they reflect, the less they feel like working.

Such people are likely to respond to even a casual remark by speculating about whether the speaker intended to insult or belittle. These people constantly ask themselves if they are satisfied—and one result is that they never are. This attitude spoils the natural joy of living and reduces the environments of such people to mirrors of their moods.

Application: If untriggered hyperreflection is your problem, you are directed not to talk negatively about yourself (the stop sign). Such a change helps to dissolve the unfortunate mixture of hyperreflection and egocentricity that are usually the basis for a negative attitude toward life.

As a guidepost in this situation, you are encouraged to talk about positive aspects of yourself and your life. If you are used to brooding, you will find this difficult to do. A Socratic dialogue and ingenuity can stimulate positive ideas. Many of the exercises in this book can be used to stimulate positive thoughts, observations, and self-perceptions. For example:

Make a list of things you like about yourself.
Make a list of things you like to do.

Guided fantasies can be used to stimulate happy recollections and memories of experiences in which you felt irreplaceable in activities or relationships. Such explorations of the positive can be done individually or in the dereflection groups described in Chapter Twelve.

Elisabeth Lukas has done much work to expand the application of dereflection. She explains:

> Dereflection means ignoring something that can be ignored and gets worse by reflection. But dereflection is more than mere ignoring, more than a distracting maneuver. What is important is not only the looking away from oneself but the observing of something that ultimately broadens the horizon and inspires self-transcendence, and the discovery of new meanings and values. Logotherapy does not entertain the illusion that the world is well, but consciously seeks what still is well, what is healthy in an unhealthy world and can be transmitted to the restless, groping, desperate human being who deeply yearns for that which is well.[1]

Hypochondria

People who are excessively concerned about their health in general, or about a specific illness, present a special kind of hyperreflection. Concern about your health is normal, even useful, because it prompts you to act when there is a problem—to see a physician, take prescribed medicine,

---

[1] Elisabeth Lukas, *Meaningful Living, Grove Press,* 1984.

change your diet, exercise, and so on. But when your thoughts are focused on your health and you keep observing yourself fearfully, then your hyper-reflection becomes an illness—hypochondria.

For such people, the helper concentrates on the second part of dereflection, the guidepost, a positive goal. Socratic dialogue focuses on a task that is important to the seekers, on something they want to do for someone they care for, or for a cause that is meaningful to them.

When you make such a commitment to someone or something outside of yourself, the importance of the illness—real or imagined—diminishes. We have all heard about a mother who rose from a sickbed to care for a child who was ill, even of an invalid who overcame disability to rescue a friend from a fire. The hypochondriac's chosen task does not need to be that dramatic to be effective. It should be consistent with the individual's values and preferences.

The efficacy for humans of contact with animals had been receiving considerable attention. John had for a long time complained about an unidentified ailment. He was fond of animals and volunteered at the Society for the Prevention of Cruelty to Animals. He benefited, and so did the animals.

Another man was experiencing fear provoked by thoughts about aging. He made a trip to Britain in search of information about his ancestry, and eventually published a slim volume about his family.

A woman whose children had all left home was focused on her loneliness and experienced all sorts of physical "symptoms." Then she discovered that a camp for Vietnamese refugees had been established in her area. She embarked on a campaign, asking friends and neighbors for old toys and clothes, which she repaired so that they could be used by the refugees.

The world around us is full of people and creatures with unmet needs. Volunteer work can be the best medicine for a hypochondriac.

Alternate List Making

Today dereflection has a much wider field of application than was origi-nally recognized. One reason may be that people who have more leisure have more time for self-observation. People pursue pleasure and are offended if life includes disappointments. They search for "the real me," for self-actualization, and do not realize that, if self-actualization is not sought with meaningful goals in mind, it can result in excessive self-reflection. In such cases, dereflection is not used primarily to find a specific meaningful activity, but rather to turn the individual away from the paralyzing feeling of meaninglessness.

For such individuals, Elisabeth Lukas developed "alternate list mak-ing." In her book *Meaningful Living*, she illustrates her method with the case of Mr. S, whose wife left him and their fifteen year old son Tom. Mr. S could do his work, but when he came home at night he could not keep himself from brooding over what had happened and how he could have prevented it.

Dr. Lukas concluded that Mr. S suffered not so much from the loss of his wife (the marriage had been unhappy) but from a general negative attitude toward life triggered by the loss of his wife. Dr. Lukas explained to Mr. S how dereflection works and asked him to cooperate in finding some activities that were meaningful to him and would dereflect him from his brooding. Although Mr. S was extremely skeptical that this would work, he agreed on a short-term experiment — he would make a list of things he had long wanted to do but had not gotten around to. Now, with more time on his hands in the evenings and weekends, he could do them. (Here the emphasis is shifted from the negative, the loss of his wife, to the positive, the gaining of time.) Dr. Lukas told Mr. S that his list would help her develop a therapy program for him based on an activity that would dereflect him from his brooding. After much prodding, Mr. S listed fifteen activities, including repairing a stove, making gourmet salads with home-made mayonnaise, setting up an electric train, helping his son with homework, and recording some favorite music programs on tape.

Then Dr. Lukas told Mr. S that each day when he came home from work, and at the beginning of each weekend, he was to select one of the activities. And he was to work on that activity, even if he thought it was useless. Before he went to bed each day, he was to make a notation next to the listing of the activity of the day, indicating how he felt: +2 for good; +1 for moderate; 0 for neutral; -1 for poor; -2 for bad. He was to do this for just two weeks. Then, Lukas told him, they would have a good idea which activities worked well for him and could be used in therapy. Mr. S was extremely skeptical. He said he knew that he would have nothing but minus 2s, but he agreed to "play this game" for two weeks.

At the end of the two weeks, he was surprised to see that after the first three days his notations began to fluctuate, with gradual movement toward the positive. During the last five days of the two weeks, he noted one +1 and four +2s.

Mr. S was proud to have helped his counselor select a therapy program. It had become obvious that setting up and operating the electric train was his favorite activity (which he pointed out rather shamefacedly). But Dr. Lukas told him that a therapy program was no longer necessary — what he had thought was *preparation* for therapy actually *was* therapy. Mr. S realized that it made no difference *what* he did — the train, the stove, the taping, and the daily scoring of his feelings — he was no longer depressed because his activities had dereflected him from brooding about the loss of his partner. The projects were meaningful to him and thus they *were* therapy, and the more traditional forms of therapy were no longer needed. The defiant strength of his human power had aroused and helped him find a meaningful direction in his life as a single father.

Dereflection makes use of a specifically human capacity: self-transcendence, our capacity to reach beyond ourselves toward meaningful tasks. Lukas comments:

> Self-transcendence is more than mere dereflection. It presents a direct contrast to that most difficult of all psychological sicknesses, egocentricity. If you think of nothing but your own well-being, you will always detect disturbances and symptoms, and no one will be able to cure you completely. True human happiness lies in the ability to forget yourself. This truth is hard to communicate to today's men and women, who are inclined to be self-centered. That makes dereflection one of the most difficult, yet most important, therapeutic methods.

Chapter Four

Modification of Attitudes

We all have problems, carry burdens, suffer pains. But the same difficulty that breaks one person may be almost disregarded by another, or taken as a challenge by a third person. It is not so much the predicament that is important as the stand you take toward it. In fact, it is often the unhealthy attitude, not the predicament, that causes distress. A change of attitude was dramatically expressed by a seventeen-year-old quadriplegic who had broken his neck in a diving accident: "I broke my neck; it didn't break me." After a period of despair, he went back to high school, and then to college where he studied psychology. He is now in his Ph.D. program and plans to devote his life as a psychologist to helping other quadriplegics.

Modification of attitudes leads you away from seeing yourself as a helpless victim (of drives, genes, environment, society, the past) and toward seeing yourself as in control, in whatever degree possible within the limitations of your circumstances. In modification of attitudes, the emphasis is on the potential of each situation, as described in these guiding principles:

- Alternatives *are* possible.
- Behavior patterns *can* be changed.
- You *can* find meaning in all situations.
- Life *has* meaning under all circumstances.
- Something positive *can* be found in all situations.
- Opportunities *can* be found even in mistakes, failures, sickness, irretrievable losses.

Attention is directed toward goals, purposes, tasks, values, freedom of choice, and responsibility, not toward gratification of drives (as in psychoanalysis) or toward mechanical processes (as in behavior therapy). The focus is away from those doors that are locked. Focus is on doors that are open or can be opened.

Exercise Draw a picture of yourself in a room with many doors. Which ones are closed forever? Label them with words or symbols. Now also label the doors that are still unlocked. What is needed to open them? What first step would you need to take to open each of these unlocked doors?

Applications

Modification of attitudes is applied principally in two main areas:

1. to change an unhealthy attitude toward life; and
2. to find a new and meaningful attitude in meaningless situations that cannot be changed.

Unhealthy Attitudes

These are always linked with negativism, resignation, despair, stagnation, indifference, and negative self-fulfilling prophecies. Unhealthy attitudes can be spotted from casual remarks. For instance, a mother may say: "With this boy I have nothing but problems. He is from my first marriage. His father was no good, and the boy is going to be like him."[1] This negative attitude toward her former husband is enough to turn the boy into a problem child. The unfortunate attitude of the mother freezes the boy in a hopeless situation. A vicious cycle is set in motion: the unhealthy attitude of the mother has a feedback effect on the boy, who will develop real behavioral problems—problems that confirm the mother's belief that the boy is a troublemaker.

Another example of an unhealthy attitude is seen in a young man who, after being fired from two jobs, says in despair: "I am no good. My brothers and sisters are successful, but I am a failure." His sense of defeat blocks all efforts of will—but only a strong exercise of will can free him from his dilemma.

A third example is a wife who complains, "It's useless for me to talk to my husband. He doesn't understand me." This attitude precludes a new beginning in communication between the woman and her husband.

Modification of attitudes redirects attention toward new thoughts and insights, toward positive, psychologically healthy attitudes. It is mostly accomplished through Socratic dialogue. When an individual has an unhealthy attitude toward life, the dialogue may provide information, practical help, or a positive perspective.

Information
The mother who blamed her son's problems on her former husband was told that behavior is influenced by parents but not in the way she had

---

[1] Examples from Elisabeth Lukas, *Meaningful Living*, Grove Press, 1984.

imagined. Characteristics, talents, and tendencies may be inherited, but not as good or bad qualities. It is up to the parents to mold the natural endowments of the child into socially desirable behavior. It was made clear to her that the boy's undesirable behavior was not predetermined by his father, and that it was *her* responsibility to guide her son's development. Her attention was shifted from an area over which she had no control (the boy's inherited characteristics) to an area where she *did* have control (the boy's behavior). This changed the self-fulfilling prophesy that "the boy will fail" to the expectation that "the boy will succeed."

Practical Help

The young man who considered himself a failure after two defeats was given information supplemented by practical help. He was told: "Each person has gifts in some areas and not in others. We'll find out, by testing, in what areas your talents lie, where you will find your place. When you know that, you can concentrate your energy on finding a job in that field and you'll see that you cannot fail." This approach rekindled his courage and confidence. Again, attention was shifted toward positive and promising areas.

List the Positive

The wife who claimed that her husband did not understand her was encouraged to make a list of her husband's positive qualities. She was amazed by how many she thought of: "He doesn't play around, doesn't drink, plays with the children, is not a spendthrift ..." Looking over the list, she said: "In a way, I can be glad to have such a husband. Of course, he's quite impossible to live with, but when I see what other husbands are like, I can be thankful." This new attitude provided the basis for counseling.

An attitude is healthy if it directs you toward goals that are meaningful to you, or if it at least keeps open the path to such goals. Such an attitude will help you pull yourself out of crises and, equally important, it may prevent them. A healthy attitude leads to an affirmative view of life and of human nature, and so it is good preventive medicine.

"Blows of Fate"

When blows of fate produce *unchangeable, meaningless situations*, modification of attitude is the principal means of help. Blows of fate are always perceived as meaningless, and rightly so. The loss of a loved person, the permanent loss of health, the effects of a catastrophe can neither be undone nor do they by themselves contain meaning. But doors are still open and modification of attitudes will help you find guideposts to them.

Persons suffering from blows of fate cannot be healed in a medical sense. But they can be comforted. Many of those blows are not caused by sickness but by a loss of value. This is experienced when a friendship is broken, a marriage fails, a person close to you dies, a professional career ends, you have a great disappointment, an ineradicable guilt, or a substantial material loss.

When you are in a meaningless situation that must be accepted, ingenuity is required to help find a meaningful attitude. Frankl cites the example of the old physician who, three years after his wife's death, still could not get over his depression. In a Socratic dialogue, Frankl asked the doctor what would have happened if he had died before his wife. The old man replied that that would have been unbearable for her. Frankl suggested that the man's suffering might be the price he had to pay to save his wife from suffering. For the first time, this client saw a possible meaning for his grief. This change in attitude made it possible for him to then begin to search for meaning in his life as a widower.

A woman whose husband divorced her was devastated. Her whole life had centered around him. During one of her sleepless nights she got up, dressed, and took a walk in a nearby park. Suddenly she felt as if a weight had been lifted from her. She took deep breaths of the cool night air, listened to the stillness, and realized that this was an experience she had never had during the fifteen years of her marriage. She became aware that many new experiences lay ahead of her. Her attention was shifted from what she had lost to what she may have gained.

A very common change of attitude is expressed in a sentence that has become a cliche. Many a mother whose daughter is getting married feels sad and bravely comforts herself with "I'm not losing a daughter, I'm gaining a son-in-law." Susan Schaub, a student at the Institute of Logotherapy, called this change of attitudes "rearranging the furniture in your mind."

A person suffering a loss can find inspiration in the examples of others—the lives of Franklin Roosevelt and Helen Keller, for people with similar disabilities, for instance. And meaning can be found in providing an example. A patient in a cancer ward, after he was told that he had only a limited amount of time to live, said to his doctor: "If you think I am going to waste the last months of my life, you have another think coming." This patient went from bed to bed and talked to others who, like himself, were incurably ill. He helped them, and he helped himself, by engaging in activity that he considered meaningful.

A teen-ager said: "We just buried Grandpa. He suffered pain for months. But when we visited him, he cheered *us* up. He gave us kids a great gift—he showed us how to die with dignity."

This youngster confirms Frankl's contention that attitudinal values provide an important path to meaning. That you can find meaning by what you experience is easy to see. What is less obvious, and still widely overlooked in psychology, is the third area listed by Frankl: You can find meaning by the way you bear unavoidable suffering. You still have an all-important choice:

You can ask yourself why such a tragedy happened to you—a question that has no answer and that therefore leads to despair.

Or, after a period of grieving, you can accept the unavoidable and ask yourself what you can do *now*, in the painful situation in which you find yourself—a question to which you *can* find answers and that therefore leads to hope.

Here are some sample questions that can accomplish the shift from despair to hope:

- Who in this situation needs my help?
- Is there someone whose pain I can reduce?
- What is the most important thing I can use my time to do?
- What am I still able to do that would benefit someone?
- Whom do I love and wish to protect in this situation?
- To whom can I give support?
- Is there some unfinished business with someone that I can settle?
- What wisdom or awareness do I have that can benefit others?
- Is there any part of my pain or experience that could be shared to benefit others?
- What do I still have that I can more deeply cherish?
- What are the first steps I need to take to implement my new attitude?

Attention shifts away from what is lost to what is still available, away from what is sick to what is still healthy, away from the area of "fate" to the area of "freedom."

A chemically dependent alcoholic has no freedom about the dependency but is free, after detoxification, to decide whether or not to take that first, fateful drink.

A person suffering from endogenous depression (a biologically caused depression that comes and goes without apparent reason) has no freedom to fight the unavoidable, oncoming attack (except by taking medication to diminish the intensity of the depression). But this person is free to lead a meaningful life during the periods of normalcy between depressions.

Elderly people have no freedom from the unavoidable consequences of old age—loss of hearing, deterioration of sight, loss of friends who die, forced retirement, and feebleness, for example. But they are free to use their assets, including experience and wisdom. A Socratic dialogue can help them to focus on meaningful activities and experiences for which they did not have time earlier in their lives. Modification of attitudes may seem in some ways to overlap with dereflection. Yet the applications of these two methods have distinct differences, pointed out by Dr. Lukas, which are summarized below:

Modification of Attitude

The goal is to correct an unhealthy attitude toward a problem over which you have no control (incurable illness, death of someone close).

The expected result is inner growth through changing yourself.

The approach is to help people gain a perspective that enables them to see something old in a new light, to accept fate with a new attitude, to search for meaning in the existing situation, to change *unavoidable* suffering into a human triumph, to motivate the individual to courage and dignity.

Dereflection

The goal is to reduce unhealthy hyperreflection over a problem that is self-induced by hyperreflection or hyperintention (such as sleeplessness or sexual dysfunction).

The expected result is inner growth that is achieved by forgetting yourself.

The approach is to help people find something new that reduces the significance of the old, to overcome egocentricity by reaching out to meaningful people and causes, to search for meaning *beyond* the existing situation, to eliminate *avoidable* suffering through self-transcendence, to motivate the person to commitment and tasks.

Chapter Five

Guideposts to Self-Discovery

In the first chapter we spoke of two kinds of meaning that will help you lead a fulfilled life: "ultimate meaning"—awareness that there exists an order of which you are a part, and the "meaning of the moment"—awareness that each moment offers you meaning potential to which you can respond. These two are interrelated. As we pointed out, you may have a healthy philosophy of life (religious or secular) that will guide you to respond to the meanings of the moment; and you may learn to respond to the meanings of the moment in such a way that you develop a healthy philosophy.

Logotherapists believe that, deep within your spiritual dimension, there is a voice that can tell you what your meaningful responses to various situations are, but that many barriers (physical, psychological, educational, social, cultural) drown out your inner voice. Logotherapy provides guideposts to the many areas of meaning. This book concentrates on five areas in which you are likely to find a source of meaning.

The first is the area of self-discovery. It is of meaningful importance to you to know who you are. Not who you seem to be behind all the masks you have learned to put on so that you will be loved, accepted, and successful, but who you *really* are at your core. From childhood you have listened to the voices of others—parents, teachers, peers, admired and beloved persons. You needed to do that to live, even to survive. But you also need to know the you behind the masks you put on. Some masks you accept, others you reject, often unconsciously. You need to know, when you are responding to the meaning offerings of a moment, if the response is yours or if it is, without your being aware of it, a response learned from your father, mother, peer, or other important person.

Approaches to Self-Discovery

It is not easy to know who you *really* are. You have a body, with its strengths and weaknesses. You have a psyche, with its impulses, drives, and instincts. You were born with a certain character that tends to be optimistic or pessimistic, extroverted or introverted, guided by thought or emotion. You also have a personality that has been shaped by your experiences. And you have a spirit that contains your essence and enables you to take a stand toward the limitations of body, psyche, character, and personality. You can decide who you are, and *who you want to become* within your potentials.

You are the total of all of these aspects. Most important is your spirit. You need to hear the voice that emanates from your spirit and guides you to meaning.

Every time you have a glimpse of your true self, you will also have a glimpse of meaning. The self you can discover is not merely the self that has developed in the past, but also the self that pulls you toward your goals. Many of these glimpses of yourself are unexpected—they may come during conversations, while you are listening to a lecture or reading a book, during meditation, or during an experience in nature or art.

A Socratic dialogue can be a *planned* attempt to gain insights into your true self. The dialogue can be a direct or an indirect approach to self-discovery.

Direct Approaches

Sometimes the direct way brings results. The question "Who are you?" is repeated over and over until the answers—after superficial beginnings ("Joe Bloke," "an attorney," "Mary's husband")—come from a deeper level ("a very vulnerable person," "a failure despite seeming successes," "an eternal doubter"). Sometimes one returns to the early "superficial" answers and explores what lies behind them: "An attorney— what does that mean to you? Money? Status? Justice? Helping the disadvantaged?"

Here is another direct approach to self-discovery: Make a list of adjectives that describe how you see yourself. Better yet, make two lists—one of things you like about yourself, the other of things you don't like. Look at the lists. Do you see anything that surprises you? Which was easier to write down, the positive side or the negative side? Are you surprised by how many things you like about yourself? Many people are surprised, since our society makes us more aware of what is wrong with ourselves than of what is right. Which of the negative traits would you like to change? Undesirable qualities often appear on the positive side as well as on the negative side. Sometimes the negative is the price you have to pay for something positive you don't really want to give up: You don't like being oversensitive and vulnerable, but you like your artistic ability. You realize that being an artist requires sensitivity. Or: You regret that you let people take advantage of you, but you like being a friendly person. But some people are likely to take advantage of friendly individuals. One goes with the other.

Indirect Approaches

Usually an indirect approach to self-discovery is more useful.

Childhood memories. What are your earliest childhood memories? They may be painful, happy, puzzling. What were your favorite stories, fairy tales, movies, radio or television shows? What were the favorite sayings of your mother, father, other important persons?

Why do you remember some trivial episodes? What was their importance? Are they still important? What is their importance today? Do these memories offer an important clue to what you are today, what your values are? Have your wishes and hopes been fulfilled?

What are your hopes now? What once was painful and frightening—is it still so? Did something positive come out of the negative experiences? Can you see meaning in those old, painful experiences?

Example:

When asked about painful childhood experiences, Erica told this story: When she was four, she knew that her mother was eagerly awaiting a letter from grandfather. One morning Erica saw the mailman on the other side of the street. She ran across, and the mailman gave her the anticipated letter. When Erica brought the letter home, her mother punished her for crossing the street. Forty years later Erica still felt the disappointment, the pain she had experienced because she was punished when she expected to be praised. She became a reserved, distrustful woman. Socratic dialogue revealed that she blamed the incident with the letter for her negativism. "All people are beasts" and "That's gratitude for you" were her favorite sayings—as they had been her father's. The "lesson" of that incident settled into fertile soil.

Erica and her helper looked at the incident from the viewpoint of the adult Erica had become. She found a different yet obvious explanation of what had happened that long ago day: Her mother had punished Erica as an expression of her love for Erica. Rushing across the street had been dangerous. And Erica's mother had valued her daughter's safety more than the anticipated letter.

Such an incident can be responsible for a turn in an unfortunate direction. Childhood emotions can switch one's life onto a new track, and adult rationality often cannot switch life back to the happier path it had been on. The episode with the mailman was probably not the only reason Erica became distrustful, but certainly it was partly responsible for the masks she wore to protect herself. Behind those masks lived a woman who longed for close human relationships. And it was not too late—it is never too late to give yourself a chance to emerge from the rubble of disappointment.

Favorite fairy tales and stories can be the keys to your real selves and they may reveal your early hopes. It is not important which tale was the favorite. What is important is how the individual interprets the favorite tale. Take "Cinderella." What does that story tell you? That some people are exploited? That even the lowliest person has a chance? That hard work and virtue are rewarded? That amazing changes are possible? That miracles occur? That you should not believe in miracles? That you will be punished if you miss a deadline? That disappointment comes when you realize that the "ball of life" does not last forever? That stepmothers are cruel? That in the end they lose? That the real prince will recognize you, even through masks and disguises? The interpretations you choose will give you glimpses into your hidden self.

A refugee from Hitler's Europe came to the United States without a cent. This man achieved self-confidence through his memories of the novels that had been his favorites in his youth—Daniel Defoe's *Robinson Crusoe* and Jules Vernes' *Mysterious Island*. When he was a child he had learned from those two books that even if you lose everything, you can rebuild your life. Here, too, the message is not in the stories, but in the interpretations that are given to the stories. As seeker and helper explore such memories with a Socratic dialogue, they will focus on the positive— even on the positive side of a negative experience.

"**If you were an animal . . .** " Another to way to probe your unconscious self-concept is to identify with an animal or an inanimate object. If you were an animal, what would you be? A mouse? A squirrel? A tiger? An eagle? If you were a flower—would you be a rose? a violet? a cactus? If you were a body of water—would you be the ocean? a rushing brook? a wide stream? You can let your imagination roam and have fun identifying yourself with a color, a smell, an ice-cream flavor, a fabric, a building, a work of art.

Identification is but one step in self-discovery. Socratic dialogue will also explore the deeper reasons for how you identify yourself. Suppose you see yourself as a mouse. What does that mean to you? Smallness? Cuteness? Shyness? Repulsiveness? An owl may represent wisdom or nocturnal exploitation. A squirrel may represent frugality, hoarding, liveliness, alertness.

You can play an identification game in a group. You tell how you see the others (which animal or flower), and then how you see yourself. The game provides a chance for self-discovery, and a chance to learn how you appear to others.

Arthur was quiet and reserved. Group participants saw him as a mole, a mouse, a porcupine. But when it was Arthur's turn to identify himself, he said he was a tiger slipping stealthily through the jungle, ready to pounce.

What's in a name? Another way to learn about yourself is to explore how you feel about your names—first name, middle name, family name, pen name, maiden name, changed name.

Does your name tell others about your origin? How do you feel about this "give away"? Does it mean anything in your language or in any other language? Are you named after someone? Do you identify with that person? Do you identify yourself with your name? In what way? Would you like to have a different name? Have you changed your name? Why? Which nickname is your favorite? Which corresponds best to your personality? How did your parent choose your name? What do you think of it? Did you fulfill your parents' expectations? Do you have a monogram on your stationery? wallet? handkerchiefs? Why? How do you feel when you sign letters? checks? documents? If you could easily change your name, what name would you choose? How do you feel when someone forgets your name? misspells it? mispronounces it? These and similar questions can help you to learn about your personality.

Nonverbal Approaches

All the approaches to self-discovery suggested above have used words. Other helpful approaches are nonverbal and use the arts. The information revealed may be useful by itself, or it can be enhanced with a Socratic dialogue.

Mask-making. Make a mask out of paper and paste and color it to your liking. Or buy a paper mask and change it to suit you. How do you feel wearing this mask? Would you like to change it? Take it off? For a while, or for good? One man made a clown mask for himself and then tore it into pieces, saying angrily: "All my life I've played the clown to get attention or approval, and all these years I've wanted to be taken seriously."

Face painting is a variation of mask-making. You can use white face cream, lipstick, and eyebrow pencil (and any other coloring you want) to paint your face—beautiful, funny, grotesque, scary, any way you want. If face painting is done in a group, you can play out your painted-on identity in how you relate to the others in the group. Does your painted face help you to know what you want to be?

Self-portrayal. Get crayons of various colors and a large sheet of paper. Now draw yourself. Not a self-portrait, but an abstract picture of lines, colors, and symbols that you put down on the paper as they arise from your unconscious. Don't think, just draw what you feel. Then talk about the results.

After drawing such a self-portrayal, one woman said, "I'm confused. Look at this jumble of lines. They are faint and fade into nothing. And so much brown and black! I would like to have strong lines leading to something, and bright colors—red and green."

The helper encouraged this woman to make a second drawing with the lines and colors she wanted. "Now hang these two drawings over your bed," the helper told her, "and look at them every morning before you start the day. The first represents your self-image as it was superimposed on you by your past experiences. The second represents your buried past that is struggling to emerge."

The line game. This game is played by two people. You can play it with your helper or with any other person—your parent, partner, friend. You face the other person across a table, with a sheet of paper between you. You take turns drawing lines, one line at a time, any length in any direction. Each of you begins on your own side of the paper. Are your strokes strong and aggressive? Vague and timid? Do you chase or avoid the other person? Do you want to drive your partner off the paper? From subsequent discussion you can learn a lot about yourself.

"I am a thing in the room." This is an exercise developed in Gestalt therapy. You pick any object in the room and identify with it and talk as if you were that thing. "I am a book on the shelf," "I am the wall," "I am the drinking glass." Then develop your theme. For example, as the book you might feel beautiful, bound in leather, orderly as you stand in place among your peers, beloved, useful, inspiring, informative; or you might feel neglected, abused, covered with dust, ready to be thrown out. As a wall you might feel important—you provide protection, privacy, a place where others can express their creativity by decorating you; or you might feel as if you are a hindrance, confining, something to keep people out; or a place for doors and windows that allow people to see and reach the outside world. As a drinking glass you might feel useful, receptive, open to all possibilities; or you might see yourself as fragile, empty, common and— depending on your way of seeing yourself—half empty or half full.

Self-Actualizing

Nowadays there is much talk about "finding yourself." The exercises above and the Socratic dialogues they produced showed you many aspects of yourself. Which aspects are you going to actualize? Obviously you will want to actualize the parts that are healthy, positive, meaningful.

It is not enough to find out what you really are and to daydream about that image. You have to *do* something about it. You may be able, on your own, to get from what you are to what you *can* be. Sometimes, though, a little assistance is required. One form of such assistance is the "as if" method developed by logotherapist James Crumbaugh. This method is described in Appendix B. It helps you to break out of an unwanted behavior pattern based on a low or unhealthy self-image. If you can break that pattern for just a moment, you will be convinced that you are not its helpless victim. For that one moment you will be what you want to be, what you know you can be. That moment of healthy self-actualization can be a turning point.

Let's say that you behave like a shy person. Everybody knows you as shy and expects you to be shy. You expect yourself to act like a shy person. The "games" that you have played with your helper have shown you that, deep within, you have the capacity to be gregarious. Now you make a contract with your helper that, in at least one situation, you will be as gregarious as you know you can be but never have had the courage to be.

Of course you don't achieve that in one big leap—and expecting to would set you up for a discouraging failure. But neither should the first step be so tiny that it does not confront the challenge. You have to stretch yourself a little toward your goal. Perhaps in the contract with your helper you can stipulate that, as a first step, the next time you are at a social gathering you will introduce yourself to one person you don't know. The second step could be that you will select a subject that you feel comfortable talking about and converse with that person. The "as if" approach will help you convince yourself that you have the capacity to actualize the self you have discovered to be meaningful.

If you are afraid to try the "as if" method, perhaps you need to have a dress rehearsal with your helper. In the safety of the presence of this trusted person, it will be easier for you to behave as you want to behave than it would be with a stranger. And a bit of humor is helpful. Humor enables you to see how ridiculous it is to behave like a mouse. Therefore, during the dress rehearsal, exaggerate your fear and planned heroics. After you have learned to laugh about yourself, it will be easier to go out into the world.

Self-actualization toward a meaningful behavior can also be achieved by a "bookkeeping" method. Suppose you have a reputation for being arrogant. Perhaps you really do use arrogance as a mask to hide a low self-image, or to hide a drive to dominate. You decide that you want to change this facade—it isn't really you. You make a contract with your helper that every night before you go to bed you will write two lists of incidents that occurred during that day. The first list will go under the heading "Today I was arrogant when I ..." The second list will go under the heading "Today I was not arrogant when I ..." After doing this for some time, you will discover a behavior pattern that you can change.

The Role of the Socratic Dialogue

The Socratic dialogue plays a major part in the process of self-discovery. The helper can use some of these exercises and games to elucidate in the seeker insights about his or her buried self. Those insights can aid the helper in finding the opening questions that can lead the seeker from the surface to deeper levels.

When the seeker suffers from self-doubt, anxiety, and despondency, the dialogue can be opened this way: "Tell me about a time when you felt self-doubt and overcame it."

If that does not get a response, the helper might try: "How about a time when you had self-doubts and felt bad about it?" This is likely to evoke the response: "I always feel bad about it." Then the helper asks for specifics: "Give me an example."

"I applied for a job as a nurse, a very desirable job. There were three finalists. I made a terrible impression. I know the woman who got the job. She is less qualified than I am, but she presented herself well."

The helper picks up the positive aspects: "You were a finalist for a very desirable job. You beat out a lot of others. You said you are better qualified than the woman who won. Doesn't that mean that you have more confidence than you acknowledge? Would you rather that you had pretended to be better qualified than you really are—that you had, in effect, lied? Was it self-doubt or honesty that held you back? Were there incidents in your life when honesty led not to defeat but to victory?"

As this dialogue progressed, the seeker might have found an answer to the original question: "Was there a time when you had self-doubt and overcame it?" Then the seeker would be turned in a positive direction and could build on the positive self-image.

Openings for Socratic dialogues are as varied as are seekers and problems. Some openings that can lead toward self-discovery are:

- Tell me something that you enjoy and do well.
- Tell me about something good and new in your life.
- Tell me something you are learning that is difficult.
- Tell me something that you have recently discovered about yourself.
- Tell me something that they said you couldn't do but you did it.
- Tell me something that you are getting better at.
- Tell me about one time when you proved that you are not helpless.
- Tell me about a time when someone expected the very best of you.
- Tell me about a feeling that you had a hard time accepting.
- Tell me about an experience that made you see things differently.
- Tell me about the time when you felt most alive.
-

  Tell me about a time you trusted yourself.
- Tell me about a time when it was hard to ask for help but you did anyway.
- Tell me about a time when you needed help and didn't get it.
- Tell me one way you have changed to become a better friend.
- What is your favorite mask? What are you hiding?

Any of these questions, any of the exercises in this chapter, or a combination, may lead to an "aha" experience, to better self-knowledge that will open a path to new meaning.

Chapter Six

Guideposts to Choices

The second area where you can hope to find meaning is choice. You always have choices, but often you are not aware of that. A situation where you don't see choices, where you feel trapped, will seem meaningless. Whenever you are aware of choices, you no longer feel like a helpless victim of the situation, and so you are able to see meaning.

As mentioned before, you must distinguish situations you can change from those that you must accept. As a rule, if you don't like a situation that *can* be changed, "the meaning of the moment" is to change it. Even in an unchangeable situation, you have a choice: you can change your *attitude* toward the situation. Aldous Huxley proclaimed that "The choice is always ours." Certainly this is true of the choice of attitude.

It is not always easy to distinguish between what can and what cannot be changed. The fateful nature of a situation resulting from death or an incurable illness, from divorce or retirement is obvious. Can a particular family or job situation be changed or must it be accepted? Sometimes a Socratic dialogue can help you determine the answer to this question.

The Japanese logotherapist Dr. Hiroshi Takashima distinguishes illnesses (and situations) that you can master from those that you have to learn to live with. A situation you can master is like a poisonous snake that is locked in a cage with you. The meaning of that situation is found in the act of killing the snake. A situation from which you cannot escape is like a strong but good-natured ox that you are locked up with. The meaning in that situation is found in learning to live with it.

Changeable Situations

Today, in our affluent and permissive society, more choices are available than have been available to any generation before now. You can choose

your major in college, your career, your partner, your lifestyle. Simultane-
ously, meaning changes during your lifetime. What seems meaningful at 18
may not be so when you are 40 or 65. To continue in a situation you no
longer find meaningful may result in frustration, neurosis, depression,
psychosomatic illness, addiction, even suicide. And in many situations you
continue to have opportunities to change.

The first step toward mental health is to become aware that you do
have choices. The second step is to determine what is most meaningful for
you at this time in your life.

The Basic List

The most direct way for you to become aware that you have choices is
for you to make a list of possibilities. From that list you can select what is
most meaningful for you.

First describe your "trap" in a sentence or two. Then list possible
solutions to your problem. Include even those possibilities that at first do
not seem practical, even those that seem ridiculous. Then list the positive
and negative consequences of each choice as advantages and disadvantages. The list will show you that you are *not* trapped, and the humor in the
ridiculous possibilities can be therapeutic.

MY POSSIBILITIES

My trap is: _____

_____

My choices are:
Choice 1 _____
Choice 2 _____
Choice 3 _____
Choice 4 _____
Choice 5 _____
Choice 6 _____
Choice 7 _____

Consequences:

	Advantages	*Disadvantages*
Choice 1	_____	_____
Choice 2	_____	_____
Choice 3	_____	_____
Choice 4	_____	_____
Choice 5	_____	_____
Choice 6	_____	_____
Choice 7	_____	_____

Look over your list and select the alternative that is most meaningful for you. You can use a Socratic dialogue to help you make this choice. In that dialogue, consider the four other areas where you are likely to find meaning:

Self-discovery. Does your choice represent your true self, or is it based on a "should," a response—perhaps unconscious—to an outside demand (from mother, peers, society)? Do not automatically reject these outside demands, but examine each one to determine if you agree with it.

Uniqueness. Consider whether your choice will place you in a situation in which you will not be easily replaced.

Responsibility. Consider the impact of your choice on others.

Self-transcendence. Remember that your choice is likely to be most meaningful if it transcends your self-interests.

Example

Max was an engineer, 35, married, with two children ages 8 and 10. He had a good salary, chances to advance, and fringe benefits that included health insurance and a pension plan. But he hated his job—the company was part of a war industry and polluted the environment. His wife shared his concern about those two aspects of his job. Lately he had begun to doubt his choice of career. He regretted not having become a teacher, so that he could have an immediate influence on the development of children. He had become irritable and depressed, suffered from sleeplessness, and had started to drink. All of this was affecting his marriage. After talking with a helper, Max wrote out his list:

MY POSSIBILITIES

My trap is: My present job
My choices are:

Choice 1	Keep the job
Choice 2	Find another job as an engineer
Choice 3	Become a teacher of children
Choice 4	Wife will work to support family
Choice 5	Get a loan
Choice 6	Find a job teaching engineers
Choice 7	Find part-time work while I study
Choice 8	Same as 7, but wife would also work part time

Consequences:

	Advantages	*Disadvantages*
Choice 1	Good salary	Value conflicts
Choice 2	Work more satisfying	Cut in salary
Choice 3	Satisfying work	No salary while studying

Choice 4	Living expenses are covered	Strain on family
Choice 5	Wife can take care of children	Financial obligation
Choice 6	It is a teaching job	Not what I really want
Choice 7	Gets me where I want to be	Reduced income in the meantime
Choice 8	Gets me where I want to be	Some strain on family

Max looked over the list and favored choice #5. However, after talking things over with his family, they decided on #8. Max, his wife, and his children made another list in which they divided the household duties. The results of these actions were not only beneficial for Max—who now had a meaningful goal—but also for his wife, who had been bored as a homemaker, and for the children, who now had meaningful tasks within the family.

The search for meaning does not end with list making. Once the choice is made, steps have to be taken to make it a reality. More lists had to be made. Max listed possible part-time jobs, and so did his wife. The children made lists of their self-chosen duties. Max looked over the colleges where he could get the education he needed to become a teacher. He began to sleep better, and he stopped drinking. "I really have no time for depression," he said.

Rephrasing

Max was willing and able to make a change. He just didn't know where to begin. Some people think they don't have the strength to get out of their traps. They are convinced that they "can't do it." If you think that you "can't do it," a Socratic dialogue can lead you to recall past experiences when you "did do it," when you did change an undesirable situation. An unguided fantasy can lead you into a future where you see yourself in a desirable situation that will motivate you to try to change your present situation. Then you can rephrase your expression of attitude, from a negative emphasis to a positive one, as seen in this sequence:

"I can't find a new job."
"I don't want to find a new job."
"I'd like to find a new job."
"I can find a new job."
"I will find a new job."

At that point it is time to take the first step from intention to reality. Make a list of first steps:

· Look at employment ads in newspapers.
· Place your own ads.

- Go to an employment agency.
- Ask friends and acquaintances if they know of any appropriate jobs.
- Apply for jobs at promising companies.
- Send out resumes to prospective employers.

Now it is time to answer ads, write letters and send resumes, and go for interviews. If you are apprehensive or lack self-assurance, the "as if" method (Appendix B) can be used. Briefly, this is how the "as if" method works: During the short time of the interview, you act as if you are as self-assured as you would like to be—and, deep within you, you are. The first impression you make becomes a self-fulfilling prophesy. When it is one of self-assurance, the interviewer responds to your self-assurance, and that response reinforces the trait in you.

Rehearsing Your Choice

Even after you have made your choice, listed the steps to follow, and learned about the "as if" method, you still may not feel ready to go out into the world and try. If so, a dress rehearsal in the form of logodrama (see Chapter Twelve) is helpful. In a logodrama, the helper plays the part of the feared "ogre." For instance, the helper can play the part of a job interviewer who has all the characteristics you fear—a person who is aggressive, distrustful, negative, and cold, someone who tries to trip up each candidate for the job. In the rehearsal, if you react the wrong way, you can change your behavior until you find a way that suits you. After this rehearsal with a helper, you can use your newly developed confidence in a job interview.

Responsible Choices

When you make choices in a situation you can change, you are likely to use your freedom in a way that suits you. And that, of course, is all right. But meaningful choice must also consider others who are affected by the choice. If you do not think about others, you may create conflicts and feelings of guilt. A meaningful choice is free and responsible. (This aspect of choice making is more fully discussed in Chapter Eight.)

Elisabeth Lukas has developed a simple form to use when dealing with a situation in which it is important to consider the feelings of others.

Problem situation: _____

_____

_____

	Consequences	
Person Involved	*Positive*	*Negative*
_____	_____	_____
_____	_____	_____

———————   ———————   ———————
———————   ———————   ———————
———————   ———————   ———————
———————   ———————   ———————
———————   ———————   ———————

Example

A woman, 35, with two children, came to Dr. Lukas with a problem that is all too common nowadays. Her husband was a good man but the marriage had become stale. The woman had met an exciting man who promised her the life she had always wanted. After the woman had talked at length about her situation and her values, Dr. Lukas had the woman make lists of people and consequences, as outlined on the form above.

Problem situation: If I get a divorce and marry my new friend, what will the consequences be?

| | Consequences | |
Person Involved	Positive	Negative
Me	_____	_____
My husband	_____	_____
Tommy (10-year-old child)	_____	_____
Sue (8-year-old child)	_____	_____
Rod (my boyfriend)	_____	_____
My parents	_____	_____

After the woman had written out the positive and negative consequences, on herself and on other people — of each possible action — it was easier for her to make her decision.

A Socratic dialogue is crucial in helping an individual who is making a choice in a situation for which there are various solutions. The dialogue helps the seeker to explore his or her innermost hopes. Here are some suggestions for opening and facilitating that quest:

- What are some of the daydreams that you enjoy?
- What makes you feel good about yourself?
- Tell me about a difficult decision you made.
- How did you do it?
- Tell me about a decision you made and regretted.
- What did you do about it?
- Have you ever had to unmake a decision?
- What did you do?
- Tell me about a decision that you made that was challenged — but that you stuck to anyway.

- Tell about a time when you didn't realize that you had made a choice, but found that you had.
- What would you like to succeed in?
- What do you wish you had tried?
- What would you like to do someday but haven't done yet?
- Tell about a time you put off something that you should have done right away.
- Was there ever a time when you wanted to say something but didn't?
- Tell about a time when it was hard for you to say "no" but you did.
- Tell about a mask you chose but didn't like.
- What do you hope your profession will do for you?
- Tell about a time when part of you wanted to do one thing and part wanted to do something else.

Unchangeable Situations

Some situations must be accepted. Then the choice that is open to you is not to change a meaningless, often painful, situation. Rather, you can choose to find a meaningful *attitude* toward a situation that in itself is painful and meaningless, like any blow of fate.

The meaning behind unavoidable suffering is not immediately evident. You need to go through a period of grieving and acceptance. Only then will you be able to ask yourself questions like these:

— What have I learned from this?
— Has it given me new tasks and challenges?
— Has it made me a stronger, more perceptive person?
— Can I use this experience to help others in similar situations?
— Can the way I endure my situation serve as an example to others?
— Does this experience make me appreciate things I have taken for granted?
— What choices do I still have?

Areas of Fate and Freedom

In any unchangeable situation there is an area of fate that you have to accept. But there is also an area of freedom where you still have choices. In the area of fate you have to find meaning through modification of attitudes, as discussed in Chapter Four. Here the choice is not whether to accept or reject the painful situation, but whether to be crushed by the cruel reality or to get comfort from some positive aspects.

Examples

A woman suffering from incurable and painful emphysema talked about how her illness reduced her participation in family affairs and her enjoyment of her children. The helper asked her: "If fate had given you a choice—to have your sickness and healthy children, or to be healthy yourself and have children who suffer from emphysema—which would you have chosen?"

A man who had lost his wife after thirty years of marriage was asked: "If you could choose between having lost your wife after thirty years and having never met and married her, which would you choose?"

These are hypothetical questions, but they elucidate meaning that is hidden by the pain of the situation. In cases of unavoidable suffering, the helper cannot cure but can comfort the seeker.

Even in unchangeable situations, there are areas of true freedom where choices can be made and actualized. Again, examples are helpful.

Examples

A woman died of cancer and left a husband and two teen-age daughters, 14 and 16 years old. The woman's death was an irreversible blow of fate. The situation that resulted contained problems that presented a need to make choices. The widower's job left him little time for housekeeping. The daughters had to go to school, shop, cook, and do the dishes. They felt as if they were trapped for years to come. The father and daughters sat down to work out this problem, and they made a list:

Alternatives	Consequences	
	Positive	*Negative*
1. Hire a cook	Little work for us	Too expensive
2. Eat in restaurants	Little work for us	Too expensive
3. Father/daughters take on various chores	Work is distributed	Each person works alone
4. All 3 go shopping shopping Saturday, cook seven dinners, and freeze them	6 "free" days	Much work one day
5. Stop eating	No work	Starvation
6. Get invitations from friends	Little work	Loss of friends

The list went on. The father and daughters had fun thinking up possible and impossible alternatives. Eventually they choose alternative #4. Each Saturday the three of them made a menu for the coming week, shopped together, and prepared and froze six of the meals, all in one afternoon. When they made the list, including even the ridiculous alternatives, they freed themselves from feeling trapped. And after they made their choice, the older daughter commented: "We don't have to keep our system forever. We can always change it."

The court denied a divorced woman, Melanie, custody of her children. This decision was, for the foreseeable future, irreversible. The helper explored with the woman her areas of freedom. During their dialogue the helper heard a logohint: This woman loved her children, but her alcoholism made her an unfit mother. Her body chemistry condemned her to alcoholism, and a single drink was too many. Where was this woman's area of fate, and where was her area of freedom? She could not change her body chemistry. But she could choose to not take that fateful first drink. Was she prepared never again touch alcohol, to make that major change in her life and so increase the likelihood that she would get her children back? Separation from her children depressed this woman so much that she sought comfort in the bottle. But the love she expressed for her children gave the helper permission to make suggestions. The helper described situations in which Melanie could use her love, not only to be in contact with children, but also to prove to the court that she was capable of caring for her own children.

The helper discussed scenarios in which Melanie would help in a nursery, a children's hospital, a dancing school, a playground, as a babysitter or teaching assistant, with pay or as a volunteer. Melanie listened to the helper's description of a day in a nursery, where she would watch the children, play with them, prepare snacks, and supervise the naps of preschool children (about the same ages as her own children). She became excited about this prospect and was encouraged to take steps toward finding such a position. Since then she has been able to stay off of alcohol. And she hopes for a new ruling on custody of her children. This is one of the fortunate cases when a blow of fate became reversible.

The Irreversible Past

One area where choice making is important is your past. The facts of your past are unchangeable. You cannot go back and redo your parents, early upbringing, past mistakes. What you *can* change is your attitude. You can take the events of your past as millstones around your neck, or as a life-belt of experience that keeps you afloat, and even as a challenge to learn and do better.

Examples

This is a true story about two women—one was lonely and unhappy, the other was surrounded by friends and cheerful. The two had similar pasts. Anna explained: "My mother never loved me. I have no role model. I don't know how to love." Mary said: "My mother never loved me. I know how bitter it is to be unloved and have made a special effort not to pass on this feeling of not being loved."

The same early experience, but with different results. Growing up unloved had made Anna withdrawn and had led to loneliness. It had made Mary reach out to others and make friends.

Anna was introduced to Mary and gained awareness that a past lack of motherly love could be a challenge instead of an excuse. A Socratic dialogue helped Anna to become aware of what had been buried deep in her subconscious—the reasons for her mother's behavior. This was an opportunity for a logodrama (see Chapter Twelve). Anna asked an empty chair on which she visualized her mother (now long dead): "Why didn't you love me? Why didn't you spend more time with me, as my schoolmates' mothers did with them?"

Then Anna switched chairs and played her mother's part. She heard herself say: "Your father was killed in the war three months before you were born. I raised all five of you children by myself. During the day I worked in a factory, and at night I took in laundry to make ends meet. I wish I could have spent more time with you. I just didn't have the strength."

Anna began to cry. "Yes, mother always was tired," she said. "But it was because she loved us that she worked so hard. She died young. I was too small to understand."

A basic change took place in Anna's behavior and in her relationships to others. The facts of her past had not changed, but her attitude toward her past had changed.

When I visited my native Vienna after 27 years, I was amazed by the fluency with which my old high school classmate, Hermann, spoke English, and even more amazed that he spoke French, Italian, Spanish, and Russian, and was learning Arabic. He was an attorney with no special need for languages. Hermann reminded me that our French teacher had repeatedly told him that he had no talent for languages. That kind of experience is, for many people, an obstacle to development, a mistake that cannot be undone, made by someone in the past. Hermann—although he did not know the term—had used his "defiant power of the spirit." For 27 years he had worked to prove that our professor of French was wrong, to prove that he did have a talent for languages. Similarly, many people live out their lives wanting to prove to their parents—dead or alive—that the parents' negative judgment was wrong. Many such people become successful in the very area in which their parents had predicted that they would fail.

Making Your Life Mosaic

To see clearly what parts of your life are unchangeable and where you still have choices, draw a mosaic of your life. Not a life map of your past, but a mosaic of your life as you see it now. Sketch your life, with symbols and stick figures to represent situations and persons. With crayons or felt-tipped pens of many colors, draw in the pieces of the mosaic: your first memories, your school years, events that had impact. How many pieces did you draw in dark colors? How many in bright colors? Are the dark ones balled together like thunder clouds? Do they have silver linings? Give each mosaic piece a name, a memory. Do you see a pattern underlying your life? Did you color some events dark because you have always considered them negative? Are they really still dark? Would you want to recolor them? You cannot change their position in your life, but you can change their colors. You may find that you have empty spaces in your mosaic that you still can fill. These are the areas of your freedom. You cannot redo the entire picture, but it is good to see what you can still do.

The Bag of Your Past

Take a paper bag and fill it with slips of paper on which you have written brief phrases signifying events in your past, such as:

- painful childhood episodes
- happy moments
- first memories
- present experiences that remind you of your past
- something you are proud of
- something you never told anyone
- a great disappointment
- a pain, fear, hope, pleasure
- turning points

You can add whatever seems important. You can dramatize this exercise by pasting the slips of paper on rocks that seem appropriate—stones that are large, small, smooth, rough, precious, common.

Then take one paper (with its stone) at a time and talk (or think) about the event and your present feelings about it. Has your evaluation of the episode changed? Has something good come from something negative? Has the significance of the event faded? Has the good feeling about it intensified? Has a bad experience lost its terror? Is what you have kept secret still worth hiding? You will realize that you have, in the past, changed your attitudes, that you can become caught in attitudes of your own making, and that you still have wide areas of freedom to change your attitudes toward events in the past.

If you are to gain meaning from a changed attitude, you may need to follow the change with action. Perhaps you cannot forget, but you can forgive. Make friends with an old enemy. Break an old pattern. Start something new that you never before thought you could do. Choices—in action or in attitudes—often require risk taking.

It is useful to examine the past from time to time, and to see where your choices are now. As Shakespeare has Hamlet say, "The past is prologue."

Chapter Seven

Guideposts to Uniqueness

Meaning Through Uniqueness

Uniqueness is the third area where you may find meaning. The search for meaning through uniqueness is different from the one that leads to the "aha" experiences of self-discovery. Your uniqueness becomes evident not so much as by what you are as by how important you are in relationships with others people or in situations.

A situation, such as a job, where you feel easily replaceable by another person—or even by a machine—will not seem meaningful to you. You will find meaning in situations where you feel unique. Of course, no one is completely irreplaceable, but there are many circumstances where it does make a difference whether or not you exist.

Creativity

One area where your uniqueness shows up is in your creativity. Only *you* can create a poem, a picture, a song, a collage, the way *you* do. Your creations may not be masterpieces, or win awards, but they are yours and yours alone. A professor of zoology expressed his awareness of uniqueness when he was asked by colleagues why he "wasted" his time collecting driftwood and pebbles, out of which he made little animals, instead of spending his time doing serious research in zoology and publishing his findings. His answer: "Any research project I do can be done by many other zoologists. But I know that if I don't put together these little driftwood creatures, no one else would make them just as I do."

More and more people are trying to overcome frustration and emptiness by writing, painting, pottery, and other artistic endeavors. These people turn instinctively to art as a self-cure for the neuroses in our affluent, pleasure and power-oriented society.

Your creative uniqueness does not necessarily have to be expressed in art. Some jobs obviously offer you the opportunity to be creative. This is true for teachers, scientists, ministers, physicians, and people in the helping professions. They can be (but are not necessarily) creative. If you use your job creatively, you are likely to feel unique, and your work will be satisfying. On the other hand, if you do your work only for the money you make or the prestige you gain, your uniqueness will evaporate and you are not likely to feel fulfilled. Money and prestige are powerful motives. But if money and prestige are an individual's goals, rather than means toward meaningful goals, feelings of failure can result.

Will, an 80-year-old man who had amassed a fortune from his business enterprise, expressed doubts that his life had had any meaning. He had always looked down on artists, and now his only son was a poet, not very successful but obviously happy. Then a friend pointed out to him that he had been creative in his own field—that he had built up his business and used his imagination, providing work for hundreds of people and manufacturing needed goods. As Will listened to his friend, his life was retroactively flooded with meaning he had not been consciously aware of before then.

Meaning through uniqueness can be found in any job. If you sell real estate, you can find meaning by making a special effort to sell to your customers the houses that best fit their needs. The same can be said of any sales job, from insurance to shoes. If you are a plumber or a mechanic, your uniqueness may lie in your creative efforts to be the best in your field. If you have a humdrum job in an office, you may find your uniqueness in your relationships with your co-workers. Or you may find it in the knowledge that you are working to keep your family alive.

Creativity is a guidepost to uniqueness and meaning. You have to become aware of this treasure and use it.

Human Relationships

Personal relationships are another source of meaning through uniqueness. No one else can relate to your child, parent, or friend the way you do. A grandfather said: "It took me sixty years to see clearly my special relationship with another human being. Ever since my granddaughter was born, she has made me feel that I am special, that I can give her the time and complete attention that not even her parents can give her."

A true love relationship is always based on the uniqueness of the other. Frankl defines love as the ability to see the uniqueness of another person, including potentials the other may not be aware of, and the ability to help the other person actualize those potentials.

Stages of Uniqueness

The Early Years

In youth, the basis for your uniqueness is created. Your first—and probably most important—special relationship is established with your mother. Others follow shortly, with father, siblings, relatives, family friends. As a child, you are naturally creative and open to relationships with others. In a nurturing home your uniqueness is encouraged, you are loved for your specific qualities. You feel that you are special.

But soon influences come into play that run counter to your uniqueness. Even in the most loving family you are expected to conform. That is when you put on masks. School places a special premium on conformity. During the teen years you struggle for uniqueness. You are supported by your peers then. But they, too, make you conform to *their* values. Society pressures you—about what you "ought" to do, what you "ought" to study, what career you "ought" to select, whom you "ought" to date and have as friends and marry. The contradictions between the various "oughts" confuse the search for meaning, and the teen years are often a time of meaning crisis.

As early as the 1930s, Frankl warned that this meaning crisis of the young can lead to the adoption of dangerous beliefs and to dangerous actions. Among the beliefs about which Frankl expressed concern are:

Nihilism: Life has no meaning.

Hedonism: Life is short. Why waste it on a search for meaning. Go after pleasures.

Pandeterminism: Certain forces—genes, psychological drives, my past, predestination, the stars—determine my life and its meanings. There is no point in struggling for meaning because something is controlling me.

Reductionism: I am nothing but an animal that can be trained, a thing that can be manipulated, categorized, predicted.

Conformity: I don't have the capacity to find meaning, and thus I do what other people want me to do—surrender to cults, gurus, dogmas.

Fanaticism: Only my path to meaning is right, and I do everything I can to force others to follow my path.

The young are not the only ones who adopt these beliefs, but they are the ones who most often express these ideas. And these ideas, which are usually difficult to counteract, obstruct the development and awareness of personal uniqueness.

Awareness of the uniqueness of another person is a priceless gift that gives meaning to the lives of both people in the relationship. Many people in our alienating society, especially children, grow up feeling that nobody cares—and that is the opposite of feeling unique. Many organizations, such as Foster Grandparents and Big Brothers and Big Sisters, try to restore human relationships that have worn thin, or to create relationships where none have existed before.

List Making

You may not be aware of the extent of your uniqueness. Perhaps, if you were asked to list your unique qualities, you would not be able to think of any. Answering the following questions may help you to be aware of your uniqueness.

- The last time you moved, who in your old neighborhood missed you? What is it about you that they missed?
- Do any of your childhood friends, schoolmates, former office colleagues or fellow workers stay in touch with you? Why?
- Who in the past has called you in an emergency?
- Who has made a sacrifice for you? In time? Money? What made each one do that?
- What have you done with your father (mother, partner, child, friend) that no one else could or would do?
- What qualifications do you put down on job applications?
- Which of your qualifications do you think convinced your boss to hire you?
- What are the reasons that your partner picked you?
- Why do people invite you to spend time with them?
- What's in your purse/wallet? Empty your purse or wallet. What do the contents tell you about your values, priorities, habits? What things do you carry with you that most other people do not carry?

A Wardrobe of Adjectives

If you like drama, you can concoct a "wardrobe of adjectives." Imagine that you have a closet full of adjectives: proud, modest, cheerful, sad, anxious, courageous, and so on. Select one of these, as you would a piece of clothing, and parade around the room. How does it feel to wear it? How does it affect your relationship with others? Does it fit? On what occasions would you want to wear it? Try one adjective after another.

These negative approaches can be counteracted by an understanding of the basic belief system of logotherapy: that human beings are creatures in search of meaning, that people want to make sense of their lives in spite of the apparent non-sense that surrounds us, that by finding meaning in our lives we can approach an understanding of the wholeness of which we are parts, that we all know deep within ourselves who we are and what we want to become and what is meaningful to us, and that we each have the defiant power of the spirit with which we can overcome limitations or learn to live meaningfully within those limitations.

Most people are willing to accept the first three paths to meaning: to discover one's true self, to determine one's choices, and to feel one's uniqueness. (More people are likely to resist responsibility and self-transcendence.) The Socratic dialogue that concentrates on awareness of uniqueness uses the techniques described in Chapter Two. Below are some approaches that you can use at any age to learn about your uniqueness:

- Think back to a moment when you felt good about yourself and the world, when things made sense even though there was reason to be confused or to feel pain.
- Make a list of the main events in your life (or a drawing of your life with its high and low points). Do you see any pattern, or was everything you experienced the result of chance?
- Remember incidents when you felt a sense of fulfillment, although you went through a painful experience, such as staying up with a friend during a crisis.
- Recall episodes in your life when you surprised yourself by acting differently from what you expected to, from what others expected of you.
- Who are your role models? What qualities in them do you admire? Do you have some of these qualities? What would you have to do to acquire them?
- Do you have a dream about your future? What stands in the way of making it a reality? What can you do to *make* it a reality?
- Tell about an ability you realize you have that, in the past, you didn't think you had.
- Tell about a situation in which you felt part of a totality.
- Tell about a moment when you took off your mask.
- Tell about a time when you were rejected because you were different.
- Tell about things that you and your parents (or peers) see differently.
- Tell about something you did for the first time.
- Have a fantasy about your future as you expect it, and a second fantasy about your future as you would like it to be. (Or draw a picture of your future life, and then change it so that it expresses what you want.)
- Tell about the nicest compliment you ever received.
- Tell about someone who trusts you.

The Middle Years

In middle age you are likely to feel more secure about your relationships, goals, and values. You have made important decisions about your career, marital status, lifestyle, and place in society. But middle age often is a time of major changes in the unique relationships (professional and personal) that once were meaningful. Your job or career, selected years ago, may have become stale. And perhaps so has your marriage. Your children have grown up and moved away. They have replaced you, at least to some extent, with their own friends and partners. You have developed doubts about relationships in which you once felt unique, and you begin to wonder whether you are going to live the rest of your life, perhaps another 30 or 40 years, in situations where you feel replaceable. Should you perhaps look for new links that express your uniqueness: a new partner, career, hobby? Your midlife crisis has struck. It's a crisis of values.

One way to sort out your values is the activities list. Make a list of things you like to do. Not things that you just *want* to do, but activities that you really enjoy. Use this list to examine your uniqueness.

- If you feel in some sense unique doing an activity, write a "U" next to it.
- If you enjoy doing an activity alone, write an "A" next to it. And write an "O" next to each activity that you enjoy doing with others. Some items will get both and "A" and "O."
- Make a dollar sign next to each item that costs money.
- Write a "J" next to each item that is job-connected.
- Write a "P" next to each item that has something to do with your partner.
- Write an "F" next to each item that is family oriented.
- Write an "S" next to each item that is connected with the society in which you live—your friends, peers, and colleagues.
- Write a "C" next to each activity that is creative.
- Write a "Y" next to each activity you would not have listed three years ago.
- Place a "W" next to those you have actually done during the past week.
- Place a "No" next to each activity that you would not want to list three years from now.
- Then select the five activities you like to do best, and label them from 1 to 5.

What have you learned from this exercise about your uniqueness? What surprises you? How many of your favorite activities are connected with your partner, family, peers? With your job? How many are creative? Do you like to do them alone and with others? Are they expensive? Have your likes changed during the past three years? Would you like them to change during the next three years? Do you really do what you want to do?

How do you feel about your list? What would you like to change? Are you in a rut? What would you have to do to get out of the rut? List advantages and disadvantages of possible changes. Couples (married or otherwise) may use this list to see how much they know about each other's uniqueness. Can you guess which items your partner will number

1 through 5? If you can, how does that make you feel? If you were wrong, how did that make you feel? How does your partner feel when you guess right? Wrong? Some people feel good if the partner's guesses are right. Others want to keep some part of themselves private, hidden from everyone.

Another exercise for exploring uniqueness (helpful for people of all ages, but especially for those at the turning point of midlife) makes use of the old fairy tale about three wishes. If you had three wishes, what would they be?

1. _____
2. _____
3. _____

What longings does each wish fulfill? What do your wishes say about where you are in your life? About your values, goals, relationships? About how fulfilled you feel now? About your hopes for the future?

By what practical means can you fulfill each of these wishes? What would be the first step to take for each? Are you prepared to take those first steps?

The Later Years

In old age the meaning-through-uniqueness aspects of life offer new challenges and opportunities. You have lived a long life, had many relationships that have sharpened your sense of your uniqueness, even if only unconsciously. Yet many elderly people feel that their lives have become meaningless. They feel useless, and as if they are treated like things instead of like unique human beings.

Many of the people in nursing homes and similar institutions feel that they have been put on a shelf to wait for death. This is also true, though perhaps less obviously so, of elderly people who live alone. These people may be widowed, and their contemporaries are dying or dead. Their busy children visit in a hurry and remember birthdays and holidays with routine gestures that give little recognition of the uniqueness of the elderly parent.

The shelving of the elderly is a new phenomenon. Until two generations ago the uniqueness of old people was appreciated. They were sought after for the treasures that come with old age—experience, wisdom, and time to be with others. For centuries children and young people who felt hurt or confused went to their grandparents or elderly aunts and uncles. Today young people with problems go to psychiatrists at $100 an hour. And Grandpa sits alone feeling useless.

One reason old people feel useless is the unhealthy value system of an affluent, industrial, materialistic society. The worth of the individual is measured in income and prestige and power. Most retired people are cut off from sources of money and prestige and power. And so society considers them worthless, and many consider themselves worthless. Modification of attitudes is required to shift from a self-evaluation based on what one *has* to self-evaluation based on what one *is*—from material goods and power to meaning.

Meaning in retirement. Retirement, when it comes, is a condition that has to be accepted. But retirement also provides many choices. Instead of brooding about what has been lost, the retired person can focus on what has been gained. You can ask yourself:

— What have I always wanted to do that I didn't have time for?
— What abilities have I acquired that I can use now where they are needed?
— What relationships have I neglected that I can now revive?
— What creative activities have I foregone that I can now turn my attention to?
— What unique knowledge do I have that I want to pass on? (This question refers to family history, identification of people in family photos, personal recollections, audio and videotapes, favorite recipes, personal skills, and so on.)

Your responses to these questions can lead to many meaningful activities.

Meaningful leisure. Many people talk longingly about retirement while they are still working. When asked what they will do when they stop working, such people are likely to reply that they will lie in a hammock, go fishing, read books, travel, play bridge or golf. All of these are legitimate leisure activities, but—unless they express something unique about the individual, these will not be fulfilling in the long run. Uniqueness in such leisure activities may be found in your relationships with other people while you are fishing or playing golf or bridge. You may satisfy a unique need in yourself with travel and reading that focuses on a long-neglected interest in a particular subject, or with retirement activities such as volunteer work.

The emphasis in meaningful leisure is not on the leisure, but on the meaning. You can use your triple treasure of experience, wisdom, and time in volunteer activities that are meaningful because they are needed. Some of those are discussed in the chapter on self-transcendence. But volunteer work is also fulfilling because your experience is an asset. Now you have time to relate to others and to make use of the wisdom you have accumulated. You can become

· the handyman of your neighborhood
· the bookkeeper, treasurer, or publicity person of your favorite organization
· a teacher of skills you have developed in your work
· a volunteer in a charitable institution (even if you have to learn new skills)

• a helper in causes in which you believe or of individuals about whom you care

Many retirees refuse to commit themselves to such retirement activities unless they are paid. They have to be led to that important change of attitudes that enables them to see that their value and usefulness is measured not in materialistic but in human terms. The ironic thing is that many elderly people lead empty lives because they will not use their skills unless they are paid. Others, who volunteer their services without pay, end up being offered paid part-time or even full-time jobs.

Older artists. It has been said that there is an artist in every child, and a Grandma Moses in every old person. This creative potential is often buried, ignored, or repressed during the so-called productive years. Many people do have creative hobbies all through their lives. Those who don't might ask themselves if they don't have some creative urges lurking within. The obstacle may be a value disorientation—retirement art seldom makes, and often costs, money.

More and more of the elderly are taking up painting, mosaic, pottery, writing, stitchery, quilting, knitting, jewelry making, or other forms of art.

• They take classes to learn or improve skills.
• They write journals, family histories, poetry, essays, playlets, cookbooks, records of their dreams, assignments for classes in various fields.
• They volunteer in amateur, and even professional, theatrical groups.
• They become gourmet and specialty cooks.
• They design and make their own clothes.
• They knit, crochet, embroider, and sew for family members, friends, and charity bazaars.
• They make puppets and entertain their friends.
• They arrange and label family photos in albums.

The list of activities available to retired people can include anything that can be imagined. Creativity does not need to be expressed in artistic endeavors. Retirees can help with the organization of businesses and clubs, they can promote causes, edit newsletters, set up mailing lists and speakers' bureaus and banquets, and they can help political candidates and causes they believe in.

Elderly persons are likely to respond to suggestions with the "yes, but" argument. They may feel that they are too old, too weak, too sick, that they cannot see or hear well, cannot walk or drive. Most older people really do have some limitations, but they also have areas of freedom in which they can make choices. There is, though, little point in telling anyone in what areas he or she should be creative. These ideas have to come from within, through Socratic dialogues that contain logohints. Occasionally an individual will find a solution without any help.

Ruth was an 87-year-old woman who lived in a nursing home. She was almost blind and unable to walk. But she suffered less from her disabilities than from the treatment she received from the staff. All of her life she had been a lady in her own home, active and needed. Now she was reduced to being considered a thing—"the broken hip in Room 27." Ruth felt a great need, as we all do, to be somebody, to feel useful. So she asked for wool and crochet hooks—crocheting was something she could do without seeing. And she began to make little caps, which she presented to the nurses.

Within days Ruth became "the patient in Room 27 who crochets for us." One nurse asked Ruth if she could make booties for her baby. Another nurse suggested that Ruth should have a little table in the hall of the nursing home, to sell what she crocheted. Ruth refused to sell what she made, but she took "orders" for caps and scarves and booties from the staff. Ruth found uniqueness in the saddest of circumstances.

Preparing for retirement. Logotherapist Robert Leslie has said that the best time to start preparing for retirement is in junior high school. What he was really saying with this startling statement is that it is never too early to plan for a meaningful retirement. You certainly cannot expect, after devoting so much of yourself during your working years to your job, to suddenly, at age 65, be able to switch to other meaningful activities. Long before it is time to retire, you have to expand your unique relationships and activities—it is never too soon to acquire hobbies, enjoy family and friends, games, travels, sports, and artistic activities. Then when your sixty-fifth birthday arrives, you will already be engrossed in a smorgasbord of meaningful activities.

Looking back. When the elderly are beginning to have doubts about their usefulness, they are at a time in their lives when there is the additional danger that they will look back and begin to doubt whether their lives really had meaning. Such doubts can easily lead to depression.

In that situation, a shift of focus is needed. The harvest of life has been brought in. Frankl warns against seeing your past as a "stubble field" of things grown that no longer are there. Instead, he suggests, when you look back you can see the "full granaries" of your life's harvest. The death of your partner cannot take away the happy times you had together. Retirement does not erase your achievements. Your present weaknesses cannot cancel the results of your past strength.

Frankl uses another simile. A person may look at the "wall calendar" of his or her life with fear and trembling. Such a person sees that "calendar" getting thinner each day as another day passes and another "sheet is torn off." Another person, as each day passes and each "sheet is torn off," makes notes on the back of the sheet about the achievements of that day and saves all the pages in a pile. That person, rather than watching the remaining calendar grow thinner, pays attention to the growing heap of experiences.

A Socratic dialogue with an elderly person concentrates on the positive and the meaningful, with special emphasis on the individual's uniqueness as seen in retrospect. This dialogue can be stimulated by family photographs, old letters and mementos. Useful questions would include these:

— Who were the significant people in your life?
— What did you admire about those people? In what ways did they help you to become what you are?
— For whom did it make a difference that you were there? In what ways did it make a difference?
— Whose existence made a difference to you?
— What were your happy moments? What or who made them special to you?
— What were your crises? What did you learn from them?
— For whom were you an example—by what you did, how you behaved, what you said?
— What qualities do you like in yourself?
— What would you say is the motto of your life?
— What one sentence would you like to have engraved on your tombstone?

Uniqueness does not disappear with age. Its expression may be limited by physical and psychological weaknesses—inability to walk, see, hear, or by depression. Opportunities exist in the areas still intact. Relationships are possible until the last moment of life. Logotherapist James Crumbaugh speaks of relationships in three areas: subhuman, human, and suprahuman. Every person can find uniqueness in one or all of these. On the subhuman level, people—and not only the old—find unique relationships with pets; on the human level we each find relationships with others, as helpers and seekers; and on the suprahuman level, many find a relationship with divinity. All of these can nourish the uniqueness of each of us.

Chapter Eight

Guideposts to Responsibility

Responsibility, the fourth area where meaning can be found, is less accept-able than the three we have discussed so far. We *want* to find meaning by personal choices that express our true and unique selves. But if those choices are not made responsibly, they will not be fulfilling. Just as pleasure without meaning is empty, and power without purpose is cor-rupting, so choice without responsibility is meaningless.

Unfortunately we are in the midst of a responsibility crisis. Although in western societies we have far more freedom of choice than our ances-tors had, responsibility has not kept pace with liberation. Frankl has suggested that we supplement our Statue of Liberty on the East Coast with a Statue of Responsibility on the West Coast.

People are free to "do their own thing" without concern for others—that is, without responsibility. They blare loud music through open win-dows, litter beaches, spray slogans on buildings, drive under the influence of alcohol, snatch handbags, rob gas stations to support their drug habits, and terrorize neighborhoods. Without commitment they marry and divorce, create children and then abort or neglect them, take jobs and then quit, change careers, hire and fire, abandon the elderly. Freedom without responsibility results in emptiness, frustration, despair, addiction, violence, neurosis, suicide.

There are three pathways to finding meaning through responsibility: by responding to the meanings of the moment; by making responsible choices where choice exists; and by *not* feeling responsible when there is no choice.

Response-ability

Responsibility can be understood quite literally as response-ability, the ability of each person to respond to meaning offerings in each new situation. The guideposts to this form of responsibility can be found in a general philosophy as described in Chapter One. This philosophy states that in most circumstances the meaningful response is to follow the values of your society—what has been found by others to be the proper response. In situations where these values don't fit, you have to listen carefully to the voice of your conscience—even if it conflicts with established values.

Example
A striking example of going against societal values to find the meaning of the moment occurred in March of 1938, when Hitler's troops marched into Vienna. That night two Jewish comedians, Karl Farkas and Fritz Grunbaüm, boarded a train to Czechoslovakia. When that train containing imperiled people reached the Czech border, an official declared that the border was closed and that the train was to go back to Vienna. While the other passengers sat in terrorized silence, Farkas stepped up to the official, slapped his face, and called him an idiot. Farkas was arrested and taken off of the train. The train returned to Vienna with the other passengers. The next day the Czech government officially declared the border closed, but decreed that foreigners already on Czech soil could remain. Farkas, in a Czech jail, was permitted to stay. Later he emigrated to the United States, and after the war he returned to Vienna and again became a popular comic. His partner Grunbaüm, following the values of society ("do as you are told"), had not slapped the official, and ended in a concentration camp.

The story demonstrates that there are moments and situations where one has to reach into one's spiritual unconscious to find specific responses to new situations. It is true that what occurred at the Czech border was unusual. It is also true that it required an unusual response.

The Drumbeat of Conscience

We live in a time of changing values. Increasingly we face situations in which individuals find that traditional responses are not suitable, situations where people have to be aware of their response-ability to go against societal values. In such situations, the individual must be aware of the voice of conscience. Conscientious objectors resist the traditional call to arms. Women reject the mandates of their churches and use birth control or abortion. Minorities, women, and the young demonstrate against traditional values; they march, as Henry Thoreau said more than a hundred years ago, to different drummers—to the drumbeats of their consciences.

How do you know whether the drumbeat is that of your conscience or of your egoism? You may find an answer by exploring the consequences of either choice:

- What are the consequences of following societal values?
- What are the consequences of going against those values? You can explore the consequences with a Socratic dialogue, list making, or unguided fantasy.
- What are the consequences of either choice for yourself and for others who are affected by the choice?
- Are you prepared to take the consequences of your choice?
- How do you feel about these consequences? How will others feel?
- How do you see your life a year from now if you have followed traditional values? If you have gone against them?
- Are compromises possible? List them. Do they offer solutions you can live with? Which one will you choose?

This is an age of crumbling traditions and changing mores. Each of us must, from time to time, choose between traditional values and individual conscience. Such conflicts *can* but *need not* lead to neurosis. How would you respond to each of the situations below?

- Your father wants you to take over the family business; you want to be an artist.
- You live with your partner; neither of you wants to get married.
- You want a child, but you are not married.
- You are married, and you fall in love with someone else.
- Your husband wants you to take care of the house and the children; you want a career outside of the home.
- You have a secure job that pays well, but you want to start a new career doing work that would provide less income but more satisfaction.
- Your old mother lives with you and has become feeble. Should you find a nursing home for her?

A New Type of Neurosis

Frankl discovered years ago that a responsibility conflict may result in a new kind of neurosis. Traditionally, neuroses have been thought to be produced by repressed trauma or past conflict. A neurosis produced by a responsibility conflict has a different source and does not respond to traditional psychotherapy. Worldwide research, reported in the logotherapeutic literature, has shown that about one-fifth of today's neurotic patients suffer from a repressed responsibility conflict—from a conflict between two sets of values, or a conflict between societal values and personal conscience. Such a conflict can also produce psychosomatic illness.

Example

May suffered from weekend migraines for which no physical or a psychological reason could be found. She had been brought up by loving parents, was happily married, had two small children and a beautiful home. Her headaches started when her older child was about three years old.

Some exploration revealed that it was at about that time that May's mother had asked her if she planned to send the children to Sunday school. May and her husband were members of a church. But her husband preferred to spend Sundays with his wife and children and friends, sailing, skiing, or hiking. May was torn between the values of her parents and those of her husband. Her Sunday headaches were produced by her value conflict. When she realized that, she became consciously aware that it was her task to respond to the "meaning of the situation" as she saw it. May found a solution to her dilemma by talking it over with her parents and her husband. And then her migraines disappeared.

Often the most important step is to realize that you have the "defiant power" to take a stand, so that you no longer feel like a victim, but instead are in control of the situation.

Responsible Choices

Meaning results from taking responsibility in situations that you can control, and from not taking responsibility in situations you cannot change. This is an important distinction, one that Frankl often described to students. He told them about Naomi, an overweight woman. She was depressed and suicidal, and she refused to go out because she was ashamed of her extreme obesity.

Frankl learned from the woman's medical records that her obesity was caused by a malfunctioning gland, a condition that could not be cured. And so Frankl talked to Naomi, not about will power and diets and exercise, but about her favorite activities—listening to music, reading biographies, cooking, having intellectual conversations with friends. Then he told her:

"You are *not* responsible for being overweight. Your body does this to you. But you *are* responsible for how you live as a woman whose body has destined her to be obese. Rock climbing and ballet dancing are beyond you—you have to accept that. But all the things that you said you like to do you can do, even if you weigh 250 pounds." Later Naomi said that those few sentences helped her more than years of psychotherapy.

This principle—that it is wise to take responsibility in situations you can control, and unwise to take responsibility in situations that you cannot change—can be applied to many predicaments. People often feel responsible even when they have no control. This leads to frustration, depression, and needless guilt. Others who take no responsibility in situations in which they *are* in control feel unfulfilled and justifiably (though perhaps not consciously) guilty.

You cannot change your genetic makeup, your psychological drives, your innate character, your society, or your past. But you can change—and are responsible for—how you live with your genetic limitations, your drives, your past. You can take a responsible stand within, even against, your fate. Mental health depends on the ability to distinguish between areas of fate (where efforts to assume responsibility will cause dis-ease, perhaps even disease) and areas of freedom (where not assuming responsibility will cause spiritual discomfort and, in the presence of value conflicts, possible illness).

Excuses

Ours is a permissive society. It has become fashionable to blame the past, the environment, and genetic and psychological weaknesses for failure and misconduct. A violent student is excused because of the jungle-like conditions of his home, an alcoholic because of his genetic makeup, a wife-beater because of his aggressive character. True, you cannot change your past, your genes, your drives. But you do control how you live within your limitations. The violent student must see that it is his responsibility not to pass the dog-eat-dog attitudes of his parents on to those around him. The alcoholic must see that it is his responsibility to not take that first drink, which will trigger his genetic response to alcohol. The wife-beater must see that while he may not be responsible for feeling aggressive impulses, he is responsible for what he does with them.

When the spirit is not blocked, when the resources of the spirit are at least somewhat accessible, you are able to exercise your will to meaning through responsible choice-making. Our society has gone far to excuse irresponsibility, especially within the family. Parents are responsible for small children. Grown children are responsible for aging parents. Couples are responsible for each other. Too many people blame "mistakes made by parents" for their own unhappiness and misbehavior. Elisabeth Lukas speaks of the "bad parents" complex that prevents many adults from taking responsibility for their difficulties. She writes: "Parents are blamed for being too strict, too authoritarian, too indifferent, too unsupportive, too protective, too demanding, too democratic, too insecure, too inconsistent." There is hardly any parental behavior that cannot be used as an excuse. When children shift the blame to their parents, the children seem to be relieved of the responsibility that really is their own.

A Word of Caution

The defiant power that enables you to change what you can control, to take responsibility when it is appropriate, lies in the dimension of your spirit and may be blocked by physical or psychological illness. When this is true, a helper—most likely a professional—must remove or reduce the block, so that your spirit will become accessible. Medical, pharmaceutical, psychotherapeutic help may be needed.

List Making

Lists can help you to clarify not only your choices but also your responsibilities. For instance, the list discussed in Chapter Six directly clarified your responsibilities. And in other lists mentioned in this book attention is focused, at least indirectly, on responsibility.

Elisabeth Lukas' five-step approach to problem solving includes lists:

1. What is your problem?
2. Where is your area of freedom? (This step requires that you list aspects over which you have control and aspects that you have to accept.)
3. List your choices within your area of freedom.
4. Which of these choices is the most meaningful to you?
5. What is your first step in the direction you have chosen?

This five-step exercise covers all three aspects of your search for meaning through responsibility. The second step eliminates the areas where you need not feel responsible. The third step concentrates on the areas where you can make responsible choices. The fourth step focuses on your response-ability to the meaning of the situation.

Logodrama

One way to bring out solutions that slumber in your unconscious is to go through a logodrama. This process is helpful in situations where you feel that responsibility is being piled on you from an outside source (for instance, mother or father— they may not be living, but their voices may still echo with "shoulds" within you.)

To explore your "shoulds," select attitudes of "important others" that still have an impact on you and which you may have misunderstood or misinterpreted.

Suppose the important other is your father. Place two chairs—one for you, one for your invisible father—so that they face each other. Sit in your chair and tell your father about your problem. Switch to the other chair and (as if you are your father) tell yourself what you "ought" to do. Then go back again to your chair, and tell your father the ways in which you agree, and disagree. By switching back and forth, you will soon become aware of your true intentions about what you want to accept responsibility for, and what you feel is not your responsibility. Sometimes an "obvious" solution will emerge that the seeker was, until the logodrama, unable to see. Jill had always wanted to be a fashion designer. But she married when she was a sophomore in college and soon had three children, the youngest only two months old. She loved her husband and children, but she resented spending all her time on child care and housework. Recently she had gone to fashion shows with a friend and had neglected her work at home, and that had led to conflict with her husband. He said that she shouldn't be going out with friends, that her place was at home. Jill argued that she was not about to make the same mistake that her mother had, that her mother had "worked herself to death" taking care of her family.

Jill sought the help of logotherapy, to resolve her conflict about what she should be doing. In a logodrama, her mother (via Jill's unconscious insights) made Jill realize that her situation was different from her mother's, and that the "shoulds" and the rebellions against those "shoulds" had to be reexamined in terms of Jill's situation. Jill thought back and realized that her father had often been sick and unemployed, that her mother had had to take on the burden of keeping the family going. Jill had an area of freedom that her mother had not had—she could afford to hire household help. But during the "dialogue" with her mother in the logodrama, it became clear to Jill that as long as her youngest child was a baby, her place was in the home—although during that time she could plan a career in fashion design that she could pursue when the youngest child entered school. After Jill had redefined her areas of freedom and responsibility, she was able to make short-term and long-term plans that satisfied her commitments to her family and to herself.

Dreams and Guided Fantasies

Dream interpretations, as discussed in Chapter Two, may contain hints from your conscience. Fantasies may be guided to the areas where, deep within yourself, you think your responsibilities lie.

Socratic Dialogue

The dialogue, by itself or in combination with other methods, is a crucial device for exploring your insights about responsibility. Below is a list of topics that can be used in a dialogue to help clarify responsibility:

- Everybody expected me to act in a certain way, but I chose another.
- I did what was expected, and felt good.
- I did what was expected, and felt bad.
- I forced myself to do something, and felt good afterward.
- I forced myself to do something, and felt bad afterward.
- I accepted responsibility and was glad.
- I accepted responsibility and regretted it.
- I learned from something I did wrong.

- No one could tell me what to do. I had to decide for myself.
- I chose something that was worth saving for.
- I decided that something was worth making a sacrifice for.
- I learned something by myself.
- I succeeded in spite of difficulties.
- I did something I am proud of.
- I finished something that was hard to start.
- I used my anger in a positive way.
- I was angry at someone and took it out on someone else.
- I overcame my anger.
- This is my favorite excuse.
- I took on a new responsibility.
- I made a promise and kept it.

These topics are, of course, only starting points, but each one can be the beginning of a valuable dialogue to discover areas of responsibility that contain guideposts to meaning.

Chapter Nine

Guideposts to Self-Transcendence

Self-transcendence is the specifically human capacity to reach beyond yourself and act for the sake of someone you care about, or for the sake of a cause that means something to you. Self-transcendence is the fifth area where meaning can be found. For therapeutic purposes, it is perhaps the most important condition, but also the most difficult to achieve.

Self-transcendence is important because it encompasses all other areas where meaning is available (self-discovery, choice, uniqueness, and responsibility), and because it provides meaning in exactly the area where you feel defeated: it turns your defeat into victory. But there is an inherent problem—how can you be motivated to transcend your instinctive ego-centricity? Why should you do anything for others, when life has dealt unkindly with you?

Think about a man who has been in a serious automobile accident. His car has been smashed by a drunken driver. His wife has been killed. He has suffered injuries that force him to retire early. Many of the relationships, activities, and conditions that gave his life content and meaning are now gone—his marriage, his work, his health. He is bitter, grieving, angry, depressed. And with good reason. How can this man be motivated to find meaning in helping others in a world that has been so cruel to him?

Motivation

The helper must use great ingenuity in a Socratic dialogue, to show the seeker that he is not expected to *forget* his self-interests, but rather to *transcend* them, to include others into his circle of self-interests—perhaps only one person to begin with. The seeker must be led to see that helping others is, in a way, "selfish," because it will help him, too. Here are some ways to seek motivation.

Logical Arguments

Logical arguments will help with people who are open to such arguments. A discussion of the world view of logotherapy may be a motivating force, and so may any other positive world view, religious or secular. The Golden Rule, in one form or another, has been a true and (unfortunately seldom) tried way to mental health.

Role Models

Role models can be another source of motivation. Which literary or historical figures or personal acquaintances do you admire? What are the qualities you admire in these people? People you admire are likely to have some self-transcending qualities. Their examples may be the first inspiration for your self-transcending actions.

Examples from Your Past

Recall examples from your past, when you helped others and felt good about it. Such incidents may range from the trivial (giving up a weekend to help a friend move) to the profound (a teacher treated you badly but you were able to transcend your resentment, and the incident prompted you to become a teacher with the understanding of children that your teacher had lacked.) While exploring past experiences, you can ask yourself:

- Was it anger about an injustice that motivated you to do something positive to rectify a situation?
- Did you learn from a painful episode and help others in a similar situation?
- Did you do some work, paid or unpaid, that helped others?
- Did you help someone even though you really didn't want to?
- Did you make a special effort to do something in which you believed?
- Did you help someone who needed your help, even though that person didn't ask you for help?
- Did you take a risk to help someone and feel good about the outcome?
- When you were in despair, did someone help you by sharing with you how she overcame similar despair?
- Did you learn to accept a difficulty by seeing someone else live with a similar difficulty?
- Did someone show you kindness when you felt you didn't deserve it?

Guided Fantasies

When the Socratic dialogue has yielded a logohint, that may lead you to guided fantasies about possible choices. The logohint may be contained in a situation. For example, the man who lost his wife and his health in a car accident caused by a person who was driving under the influence of alcohol may be led to see himself:

- promoting legislation against drunk drivers
- starting a grief group for widows and widowers, to help them face, share, and heal their pain
- starting a group or an organization that helps people who have been forced into early retirement
- joining or starting an organization that helps people who have physical handicaps to find independent work
- joining an activity that is important to him and that he had neglected because his work and home life did not leave him enough time

No Way But Up

Sometimes the motivation lies in the despair. You are at the end of your wits, you have tried everything, and nothing has helped. So you tell yourself: "I know this so-called self-transcendence won't do any good, but what do I have to lose?" So you make a list—at the prompting of your helper—of all the things you could do to help someone or some cause. You pick one activity that has some appeal and take the first hesitant step toward that goal. You hold out a hand, and it just may be that your gesture will be received with gratitude. This step often requires R-A-P: Risk (of being rejected, ridiculed, mistrusted); Action (not just thinking about something, but doing it); and Patience (success may not immediately be evident). If, after an honest attempt, this way does not seem right, you can go back to your list and pick another alternative.

Accepting the Challenge

Some people are able (perhaps with the guidance of a helper) to see the challenge hidden in a blow of fate. The easy life often seems empty, and meaning comes with the challenge to turn defeat into victory. Edward Wilson was a student of English literature at Harvard. He had a brilliant mind that made studying so easy that he was bored. He saw no meaning in life, and in a dark moment shot himself. When he regained consciousness, he realized that he had failed to kill himself, but that he had blinded himself. While he lay in the hospital he saw that with this handicap, studying—and life—would be challenging. Wilson became a teacher and an inspiration for especially gifted students.

Many people are resistant to reaching beyond themselves to find satisfaction. But it is worth the effort, because self-transcending behavior helps you to see the three-dimensional fullness of your person: Your body and your psyche may be damaged but your spirit is healthy. The self that is being transcended is the body/psyche part of you. The self that is transcending is your spirit. Self-transcendence makes you aware that what you *are* (your spirit) can win over what you *have* (your body and psyche). This awareness opens you up to meaning potentials.

Activities

Many people have difficulty motivating themselves to reach out to others or to make a commitment to a cause as they search for meaning in their lives. Many self-transcendent activities are unpaid, at least in the beginning, so a change in values may be required for participation in such activities. The woman who devotes her time to promoting legislation against drunk drivers, or the man who grieves for his wife and forms a support group for other widowers, won't get paid for their efforts. Such volunteer work occasionally leads to paid employment. But, paid or unpaid, these are fulfilling activities.

Such self-transcending actions approach meaning from all the directions mentioned earlier. They promote *self-discovery* by releasing your best innate human qualities—qualities you might not have discovered if you had followed the pleasure-and-success ways of our society. *Choice* is, of course, crucial, and all the more meaningful because it includes two more paths to meaning: *uniqueness* and *responsibility*.

The tragedy you experience makes you uniquely qualified to help others in similar situations. A brilliant doctor may try to convince a patient in a wheelchair that she can still find meaning in life. But a person in a wheelchair or on crutches who is able to say "I know how you feel—I went through the same trauma myself, and I have found strengths I never suspected I had" will be more convincing than the doctor. A quadriplegic said: "I don't want to be called physically handicapped. I am physically *challenged*."

Alcoholics Anonymous has long made use of the fact that few people are able to help alcoholics as well as those who have overcome an addiction. Similarly, the blind can help others without sight, and the incurably ill can help others in the same situation. Volunteer organizations and action groups are full of people who help where they were hurt. They may have been discriminated against because of color, race, religion, or sex, or lost loved ones to cancer, emphysema, or AIDS. The choice of self-transcendent activity must be made by the seeker. The helper can suggest possibilities after the seeker has given some logohints. Human beings are capable of amazing behavior, both planned and spontaneous. We have all read of the murderer in prison who risked his life to save other inmates from a fire, of the mother who lost a child in a senseless accident and volunteered her child's organs to save the life of another child. Logotherapists have reported deeds that no one would dare to suggest, but that patients have chosen. Dr. Takashima, director of the Tokyo Institute of Logotherapy, describes a girl born without arms—she learned to paint with her toes, and inspired other children with similar handicaps. Viktor Frankl writes of several people who transcended their tragedies and turned those experiences into triumphs. Here are three incidents Frankl mentions in his speeches.

An inmate in a Florida prison found Frankl's *Man's Search for Meaning* in the prison library. After reading this book, the prisoner wrote to Frankl, saying that he wanted to establish self-help groups within the prison, so that he and other inmates could discuss the book and talk about their lives after release from prison. Frankl encouraged this man, who overcame the doubt and heckling of fellow inmates and formed a group of recidivists (like himself). The group continued to meet even after the men were released. As a result, all but one of those men stayed out of prison.

A Jewish woman wore a bracelet with the milk teeth of her children. "This one is Miriam's," she said. "This is Samuel's, and this one is from Sarah." She had a tooth from each of her nine children who had died in concentration camps. When asked how she was able to wear such a bracelet, the woman replied simply, "I am now the director of an orphanage in Israel."

A man who had no family worked as a garbage collector in a medium-sized city. His situation certainly seemed to limit the likelihood that he would find meaning in his life. But he did. From the trash that he collected this man took broken toys, and he spent his evening fixing them. Then he took the toys to a children's home in a slum in the city where he lived—he was Santa Claus all year round.

Self-transcendence, under much simpler names such as friendship or good will, is an unconscious but important aspect of the lives of many people. A woman in an old-age home, suffering from arthritis but able to drive her car, transports others in the home to church and doctor and grocery store. A recent widower fills his empty time baby-sitting for a single mother who needs to go to work. A man lying in the hospital with an incurable disease is visited separately by his best friend and the friend's son. Father and son have been feuding for years, and their sick friend makes it his business to reconcile them. A retired woodworking teacher, whose hands are no longer steady enough for him to work, makes his tools and garage workshop available to kids in his neighborhood.

People who have suffered blows from fate are not the only ones who find meaning through self-transcendence. A growing group in our affluent society is made up of people who feel empty—not because they have lost something, but because they have everything. They are "birds in golden cages," trapped in their affluence. Albert Schweitzer speaks of a moral principle he calls "good fortune obligates"—people who have everything have an obligation to help those who have little or nothing.

Elisabeth Lukas applies this principle in her therapy. She illustrates this with an incident about two drivers on a freeway. One has an accident, drives into a ditch, smashes his car, and is hurt. The other driver, unhurt, has the obligation to help. Here responsibility and self-transcendence come together.

Many people who are not required to work—people who are wealthy or retired—feel useless, empty, depressed, and neurotic, and they are apt to become addictive. This situation challenges such people to find commitments. The world is full of people who need help and causes worth supporting, not just in the Third World but also in our own First World. Frankl concluded a talk with this sentence: "To the extent that the First World sees its task as fighting hunger in the Third World, it helps itself to overcome its own meaning crisis: we give them bread, they give us meaning—not a bad bargain." Meaning through self-transcendence is usually not as dramatic as the examples presented. It is the stuff of daily life and available to all age groups.

Until recently children helped their parents in the home, on the farm, or in the workshop. This help has become unnecessary, even impossible. Consequently, children feel unneeded and bored. They passively watch television and play with purchased mechanical toys, activities that feed the desire for pleasure but not the need for meaning. Children can still help their parents, especially in homes where both parents have jobs. Children can take care of small siblings. They can provide companionship for grandmother or a lonely neighbor. They can do many of the simple, repetitive chores that consume precious time, such as setting the table, sweeping and vacuuming, doing the laundry.

Lukas reports on an experiment she did with a group of destructive children. Usually these children played with purchased toys that they quickly unwrapped, broke, and threw away. She had the children *make* toys. They designed and constructed simple machinery, carved boats from blocks of wood, and made rag dolls with faces they painted, clothes they sewed, and hair they made from yarn. These children did not break the toys they had made. And they proudly shared those toys with other children.

At the other end of life, the elderly can use their triple assets—experience, wisdom, and time-at-hand—to find meaningful activities and relationships. Bored children, adults who chase pleasure and money, and the "useless" elderly can find meaning in reaching out for each other within and beyond the family.

Self-transcendence as a road to meaning is available to everyone, in all circumstances and at all ages. Its value is most dramatically evident for people who are suffering from meaningless pain and grief. But self-transcendence is also achieved by anyone who stays up with a friend, takes a neighbor to the hospital, visits someone who is sick, invites a new neighbor over for coffee, or does any of the kindnesses that come naturally.

Chapter Ten

Values

Values are the traffic signs on your journey through life. They say "stop" and "go" and "yield" and "wrong way." They warn that the road has a "sharp turn" or "children crossing" or that it is "slippery when wet." Values, like road signs, are useful, even life saving, and ordinarily you obey them automatically. Frankl calls values "universal meanings,"—what people in standard situations have found to be meaningful responses. Values make it unnecessary for you to decide what is meaningful in a specific situation. You simply follow the "road signs" established by parents, teachers, religious or secular leaders, government, peers, society.

But this convenience has a price. Values can contradict each other. The values of your parents may say "no sex before marriage." Those of your peers may say "waiting until marriage is silly," or even "marriage is silly." You may hear contradictory value statements about a woman's place at home and at work, about having children, abortion, homosexuality, career, participation in community and civic affairs.

There is also the possibility that your conscience may give you conflicting messages in an unusual situation. For example, if you are driving your wife, who is in labor, down an empty road toward the hospital, you might drive right through a stop sign. Or you might stop at a green light because an old man is limping across the road. The artist who refuses to take over his father's business is heeding his own values and ignoring his father's values. The man who lies down in front of a train that is carrying nuclear weapons is expressing his own values and is clearly expressing his disagreement with the values of his society. The man who refuses to pay taxes because he disapproves of how his money is spent (Henry Thoreau, for example, did not want his money spent to support slavery) is acting on his values and opposing those of his government.

Individuals who follow their consciences, rather than the accepted values of family, society, or government, must accept the consequences of their decisions. The artist who did not go into business might have to live in poverty. The man who lies down in front of the train might be run over and injured or killed by the train. Thoreau spent time in jail for refusing to pay taxes.

There are also psychological risks in being caught between conflicting values. The most widespread of these risks is what Frankl calls the "noogenic" neurosis—a neurosis that originates in the individual's noetic, or spiritual, dimension where decisions are made. A noogenic neurosis is the result of two values pulling in two different directions. The logotherapeutic cure for a noogenic neurosis (which may cause depression and psychosomatic illness) is to decide which of the conflicting values is meaningful for you. To do that, you need to explore three things:

1. Which of the values is higher in your hierarchy of values?
2. Where does each of the values come from? (parents? society? peers?)
3. Which of the conflicting values is consistent with what your conscience tells you?

Your answers to these questions do not indicate that some values are better or worse in a moralistic sense; nor do they tell you whether it is better or worse if these values come from an outside source or from within yourself. But your answers do show you that it is healthy for you to know where your values come from and, if they come from outside, whether you agree with them. Following outside values may have unhealthy consequences if you are not aware that you are repressing your own values—that you are doing something because you feel that you "ought" to do it, without being aware that you are carrying this "ought" from long-forgotten advice slumbering in your unconscious. Such conflicts of value and conscience can lead to psychological diseases, and even to physical diseases. These conflicts need to be clarified and resolved.

Clarifying Your Values

Part 1: List of Values

Below is a list of twenty values. Read it and mark the five items you think are most important to you and the five you think are least important to you. (This list is from the work of the logotherapist James C. Crumbaugh: *Logotherapy—New Help for Problem Drinkers*, Chicago: Nelson-Hall, p. 107.)

Table 1: Values

For me a high value is:
1. to be wealthy
2. to have lasting friendships
3. to have physical sex
4. to have a good name
5. to be remembered favorably after death
6. to gain romantic love
7. to be a great leader of people
8. to be healthy
9. to be a hero or heroine
10. to be of great service to people
11. to be famous
12. to be physically powerful (men) beautiful (women)
13. to be an intellectual genius
14. to find adventure and new experiences
15. to be happy
16. to understand the mystery of life
17. to fulfill religious goals
18. to have peace of mind
19. to gain social acceptance and belonging
20. to gain a personal identity

Part 2: Your Value Hierarchy

On the next page you will find a selection sheet. The numbers on that sheet refer to the values listed in Part 1 (1 = to be wealthy, 2 = to have lasting friendships, and so on). The columns on the selection sheet give you the opportunity to compare each value with every other value. In each pair listed, circle the value you consider the higher of the two.

For example, in the first column, the first line asks you to choose between 1 and 2, between wealth and friendship. If you consider being wealthy more important than having lasting friendships, circle the 1; if friendship is more important, circle the 2. Make this comparison and choice with every pair in all the columns. The columns become shorter because values have been compared in previous columns. The last column consists of only one pair (19—to gain social acceptance and belonging, versus 20—to gain a personal identity).

Now go over the entire list, add all the circled 1s, and enter the total in the box under the first column. In this instance you will find all circled 1s in the first column. This is not so for the other numbers. For number 11, you may find circled 11s in column 11 and also in previous columns. Add them all up and enter the total in the box under 11 (indicating how much you value fame). When you get to the last column, you will have to go through all the previous columns to find all the other 20s you have circled. When you have done that, enter the total under column 20.

Table 2: Selection Sheet

1-2	2-3	3-4	4-5	5-6	6-7	7-8	8-9
1-3	2-4	3-5	4-6	5-7	6-8	7-9	8-10
1-4	2-5	3-6	4-7	5-8	6-9	7-10	8-11
1-5	2-6	3-7	4-8	5-9	6-10	7-11	8-12
1-6	2-7	3-8	4-9	5-10	6-11	7-12	8-13
1-7	2-8	3-9	4-10	5-11	6-12	7-13	8-14
1-8	2-9	3-10	4-11	5-12	6-13	7-14	8-15
1-9	2-10	3-11	4-12	5-13	6-14	7-15	8-16
1-10	2-11	3-12	4-13	5-14	6-15	7-16	8-17
1-11	2-12	3-13	4-14	5-15	6-16	7-17	8-18
1-12	2-13	3-14	4-15	5-16	6-17	7-18	8-19
1-13	2-14	3-15	4-16	5-17	6-18	7-19	8-20
1-14	2-15	3-16	4-17	5-18	6-19	7-20	
1-15	2-16	3-17	4-18	5-19	6-20		
1-16	2-17	3-18	4-19	5-20			
1-17	2-18	3-19	4-20				
1-18	2-19	3-20					
1-19	2-20						
1-20							

9-10	10-11	11-12	12-13	13-14	14-15	15-16	16-17
9-11	10-12	11-13	12-14	13-15	14-16	15-17	16-18
9-12	10-13	11-14	12-15	13-16	14-17	15-18	16-19
9-13	10-14	11-15	12-16	13-17	14-18	15-19	16-20
9-14	10-15	11-16	12-17	13-18	14-19	15-20	
9-15	10-16	11-17	12-18	13-19	14-20		
9-16	10-17	11-18	12-19	13-20			
9-17	10-18	11-19	12-20				
9-18	10-19	11-20					
9-19	10-20						
9-20							

17-18	18-19	19-20
17-19	18-20	
17-20		

Look at the numbers in the twenty boxes on the selection sheet. They show your value hierarchy. How does this compare with your off-the-cuff estimate in Part 1? What surprises you in this evaluation? What are the five highest and five lowest values in Part 2? Do they match your evaluation from Part 1? Does your hierarchy give you any insight into yourself? Is there anything you would want to change? What would you have to change in your lifestyle or habits to reflect a change in your value hierarchy? Are you prepared to make this change, or are you satisfied with your present lifestyle and habits? Each of these questions can be used to start a Socratic dialogue.

Part 3: Where Do Your Values Come From?

The twenty values in Table 1, and seven possible sources of those values, are listed in Table 3. Next to each value, indicate with a checkmark what you believe to be your source or sources of that value.

Table 3: Sources of Values

Self	Mother	Father	Religion	Society	Peers	Education		
							1.	To be wealthy
							2.	To have lasting friendships
							3.	To have physical sex
							4.	To have a good name
							5.	To be remembered favorably after death
							6.	To gain romantic love
							7.	To be a great leader of people
							8.	To be healthy
							9.	To be a hero or heroine
							10.	To be of great service to people
							11.	To be famous
							12.	To be physically powerful (males) beautiful (females)
							13.	To be an intellectual genius
							14.	To find adventure and new experience
							15.	To be happy
							16.	To understand the mystery of life
							17.	To fulfill religious goals
							18.	To have peace of mind
							19.	To gain social acceptance and belonging
							20.	To gain a personal identity

This list, too, can be used to initiate a Socratic dialogue. What surprises you about your answers? How do you feel when you see that you often (or seldom) follow the values of your father or your mother? That you often (or seldom) follow your own values? That your choice often (or seldom) coincides with a value that comes from an outside source? Would you like to change? In which direction? What would you have to do to make such changes? What prevents you from making those change?

What is important for your mental health is not so much a change in your value hierarchy as your awareness of what your value hierarchy is like and where your values come from. Many people go through life with unconscious and bothersome "oughts." Those oughts create guilt and conflicts that cannot be overcome until the individual sees the value conflicts clearly and is able to do something about them. Remember that value conflict *may* but *need not* lead to problems—that *it is in your power* to resolve those conflicts. To do so, you need to know the sources of your value conflicts.

Exercises

Values are expressed in activities and experiences. As you go through these activities and experiences, difficulties arise from conflicts between your own values and those of your parents that you carry (often unconsciously) within yourself. The exercise in Table 4 explores this collision in some depth. Read through Table 4 and then fill it out.

Table 4: Value Conflicts

List three episodes during the past week when you acted like your father:	Do you agree with the values expressed by these actions?	If "no," what values do you prefer?
_____	_____	_____
_____	_____	_____
_____	_____	_____

List three epi-
sodes during the
past week when
you acted like
your mother:

Do you agree
with the values
expressed by
these actions?

If "no," how
would you want
to change?

In general, in
what way do you
act like your
father?

Do you feel good
about it?

If "no," how
would you want
to change?

In what way do
you act like your
mother?

Do you feel good
about it?

If "no," how
would you want
to change?

In what way are
you different
from your
father?

Do you feel good
about it?

If "no," how
would you want
to change?

In what way are
you different
from your
mother?

Do you feel good
about it?

If "no," how
would you want
to change?

Exercise 4

List areas of your life in which you find satisfaction, and draw a picture of how those areas fill the circle of your life. For example:

- How much do these activities and experiences fill your life?
- Where and how much do they overlap?
- How do you feel about the relative size (importance) of each of these areas of your life?
- How would you fill the empty space?
- What areas would you like to diminish? eliminate? expand? add?
- Draw another picture of your life as you might have drawn it ten years ago. Do you like it better? worse? the same?
- Draw a picture of your life as you would like to draw it ten years from now.
- What can you do to change the picture from the way it is to the way you would want it to be?
- What would the first step be toward change?

Exercise 5

- What do you *have* to do during the next week (month, year)?
- What do you *want* to do during that time?
- What benefits do you get from the things you *want* to do?
- Suppose you could substitute one thing you want to do for one you have to do. What would your life be like?
- Write down five meaningful experiences in your life. Why do they stand out? Why are they valuable? What values do they represent? Were they positive or negative at the time? Has your evaluation of them changed? What have you learned from them?

All these exercises will provide material for discussion. Other topics that can be productive include:

- Name two values important to you that contradict each other.
- Remember an occasion when you took a position you really believed in.
- Remember an incident when you were criticized for something you did or said. How did you feel? What did you do?
- What qualities do you look for in friends?
- What quality in yourself have you only recently discovered?
- Name people who have influenced you. What were the reasons?
- What was the best thing that happened during the past year between you and a friend (family member, boss, teacher)?

Horizontal Values

The Czech logotherapist Stanislav Kratochvil describes two extreme value orientations: one is pyramidal, the other horizontal. In a pyramidal value structure, one value is on top and dominating, while the other values are much less important. The man who lives only for his career, the woman who lives only for her family—these people have pyramidal value orientations. The man is fulfilled by his work, the woman by her family. But what will happen when the man's career ends with retirement, when the woman's family changes, when the children grow up and leave home, when divorce or death break family ties?

Each of these people has lived with a single central focus. Each risks losing that focus. When that happens, the value structure in each of their lives will collapse, and their lives may seem empty. Then it is difficult for the individual with a pyramidal value structure to find new areas of fulfillment. Such sudden emptiness can lead to sickness, even to premature death.

The individual with a horizontal value orientation has several value areas that exist parallel to each other—career, family, friends, hobbies, creative activities, special interests, faith. If one value fades, many others remain. The man whose career ends, the woman whose family ties collapse in a midlife crisis, can find meaning in other activities representing other values of similar importance. Horizontal values are insurance against an empty life.

Most people have value orientations somewhere between these two extremes. It is good preventive therapy to widen the circle of interests during the earlier stages of life, especially if you seem to have pyramidal values. A horizontal reorientation will enable you to perceive wide possibilities for meaning, and will prevent you from developing spiritual blinders.

Chapter Eleven

Meaning in Marriage and Family Life

The meaning of the moment is different for each person in each situation. Thus, there is no meaning for an entire family as a group. There is, however, meaning for each family member, including meaning in their relationships with each other.

Meaning for Family Members

Most of the methods and exercises mentioned in this book—Socratic dialogue, dereflection, modification of attitudes, list making, logodrama, fantasies, exploration of values—can be used for individual members of a family.

Marriage and family counseling offers opportunities for additional methods. In *list making*, for example, the husband is asked to write down what he likes and dislikes about himself, and the wife is asked to make a similar list about herself. Each is then asked to guess what the partner's list contains. The guesses are then compared with what the partner really put down. Were the guesses mostly right? Wrong? How well do they know each other? How does one partner feel if the other guessed correctly? incorrectly? Different couples are likely to have different reactions. Some couples feel good if their guesses reveal understanding of each other. Others feel uncomfortable. In some cases, one partner will feel good, the other will feel bad. What does this say about their relationship? Socratic dialogues, first between each partner and a helper, then between the two partners, will help them to see what their reactions say about their relationship.

This mutual list making can also be tried with parents and children, between siblings, or with any family members, such as grandmother or uncle, who live with the nuclear family or have close relations with it. How does a son feel if he is not (or "too well") understood? What does the grandmother come to understand about her role in the family?

As was discussed in the previous chapter, a guessing game can also be played in which the members of a family establish their value hierarchies. Marriage partners and other family members need not have the same, or even similar, value preferences. But it is healthy for them to know what values are most important to the people with whom they live.

Another method that is useful in family counseling is *logodrama*, which provides family members with an opportunity to talk with each other. It is best to take one problem at a time. When the dialogue moves on the old tracks and a collision seems unavoidable, one partner is asked to sit in the chair of the other and to answer the way he wished she would have answered. For example, here is a dialogue between two people on a collision course:

> *She:* I am fed up with your working late hours.
> *He:* Do you think I enjoy it?
> *She:* Obviously you enjoy it more than spending the evening with me. You probably have a girl friend.
> *He:* You're crazy. I work and work, and you accuse me of having an affair.
> *She:* I have my reasons. Didn't I catch you with Susan?
> *He:* And how about you and Harry?
> *She:* That only happened because you left me alone every evening.

Mutual accusations have a tendency to snowball into an avalanche. The helper suggests that the partners switch chairs and that the husband, sitting in his wife's chair, answer for her.

> *He:* (speaking for his wife) I'm sorry you have to work so late. I would like to be with you more often.
> *He:* (changing chairs again and now speaking for himself) I'd like to be with you more, too. But I don't mind working overtime because this way we can afford a vacation together.
> *He:* (switching to her chair and again speaking for her) I appreciate that, darling. Vacations mean so much to me.
> *She:* (speaking for herself) Vacations *do* mean a lot to me. I guess it's true that we couldn't have them unless you worked a lot of overtime.

The collision has been avoided. The couple goes on to speak of other problems.

> *He:* Susan really was an exception. You were on vacation by yourself and I felt lonely.
> *She:* I know what you mean. It was like that with Harry. I was alone so many evenings.
> *Helper:* What could you do so that things like that won't happen in the future? What possibilities do you see?

The couple makes a list:

- They will give up the shared vacation and spend evenings together.
- The wife will go to evening classes that interest her while the husband works overtime.
- The wife will work part time to earn money for vacations and other extras.
- They will continue as before and fight.
- They will get a divorce.
- They will reduce other expenses so that they will not need overtime pay for vacations.

The advantages and disadvantages of each of these alternatives are discussed. The couple chooses the idea of an evening course for the wife. She has long wanted to make pottery. The wife also expresses an interest in looking for part-time work that appeals to her—she does not want to work just for the money.

Often marriage and family problems seem difficult to solve because the partners talk *past* each other instead of *to* each other, or because their conversations disintegrate into accusations and defenses that block communication. When people talk past each other, "echo talk" can be used. *Echo talk* uses the simple rule that each partner may answer only after he or she has repeated the partner's statement to the partner's satisfaction.

> *She:* You are a blockhead and turn everything I say around to suit you.
> *He:* That's a lie. You yourself . . .
> *Helper:* Stop! That's against our rule. First repeat what your wife said.
> *He:* "You are a damned blockhead and must always be right."
> *She:* That's not what I said.
> *He:* But that's what you meant.
> *She:* How do you know what I meant?
> *Helper:* Do you remember what your wife said?
> *He:* Of course. I'm not an idiot. "You are a blockheaded fool and turn around everything I say to suit you."
> *She:* I did say blockhead, but nothing about fool. You're not a fool.

He: Well, thanks. At least there's something good about me. (He laughs.)

She: Oh, you have your good points all right.

Helper: (to husband) What's your response to being called a blockhead?

He: I have my own opinions, yes, but I don't turn anything around.

She: You do, too. Do you remember ...

Helper: Echo, please.

She: "I have my own opinions, but I don't turn anything around."

He: Yes.

She: Remember last year, when I admired the pearl necklace in the shop window, you said accusingly that I am ruining you.

He: "Remember last year, when I admired the pearl necklace, you accused me of ruining you."

She: Yes.

He: Well, if that's all you remember ... Once a year it's all right to turn things around, isn't it? (They laugh.)

Again, they have switched tracks. They are no longer arguing against each other—they are laughing together. The way has been opened for a dialogue.

The *flashlight* technique is used when the discussion begins to become aggressive. Elisabeth Lukas has worked out some rules for this method. The couple and the helper sit together. The helper does not participate in the talk, but is merely an automatic control, holding a flashlight and lighting it whenever one partner says something offensive to the other. When the flashlight lights up, the person who is speaking must repeat what he or she just said, but this time without hostility, sarcasm, name-calling, blaming, or negativity. Then the discussion continues. Only one person speaks at a time, and the rule with the flashlight is applied equally to all.

Here is an example of a discussion in which the flashlight technique is used:

She: You are a blockhead and turn everything I say around to suit you. (The flashlight lights up.)

She: You have your own opinions and don't listen to what I'm saying.

He: I do listen, but you usually babble nonsense that doesn't interest me. (The flashlight lights up.)

He: I do listen but I am not interested in your gossip. (Flashlight lights up.)

He: All right, then. You often talk about things that don't interest me.

She: Then say that to me. I can't read your thoughts, Mr. Professor. (Flashlight lights up.)

She: I can't read your thoughts.

He: All right, from now on I'll tell you. But you mustn't jump all over me, the way you do every time I ... (Flashlight lights up.)

He: You mustn't resent it.

Slowly the atmosphere becomes less poisonous and a true dialogue becomes possible.

The WAMFA Game

Another method for keeping marital discussions factual and preventing them from become emotional is based on marriage-counseling techniques first used by Father Gabriel Calvo of Spain. His method has been adopted by therapists with widely differing perspectives, and it can be used with a logotherapeutic slant. The method is called the WAMFA game. The letters in this acronym stand for What Are My Feelings About? This game is most useful as a self-help tool for couples who see the first storm signals and want to avoid a shipwreck, and for couples who are in good marriages that they want to make even better.

A session of the *WAMFA* game takes about half an hour. It can be played every day as an exercise of the spirit, or it can be reserved for times when a special problem comes up. If you play it every day, select one problem for each day. One day the game might deal with the small irritations of marriage (*WAMFA* having to pick up after you?), with serious conflicts (*WAMFA* your refusing me when I want to have sex with you?), or with general, rarely discussed topics (*WAMFA* our love for each other?). The game has four parts that can be summed up in the word WEDS, which is an acronym for:

*W*rite for ten minutes about your feeling on the selected topic.

*E*xchange what you have written, and each read what your partner has written.

*D*ialogue with your partner for about ten minutes about what you have each written and how you each feel about what you have read.

*S*elect a topic for the next day.

The *WAMFA/WEDS* method focuses attention on present feelings, instead of exploring the deep-seated causes of a problem ("Your mother has always cleaned up after you. I am not your slave. Clean up your own mess." Or "If you yell at me all day, I can't have sex with you at night.")

Each partner states the problem clearly. What does the husband feel when his wife leaves his socks on the floor? What does the wife feel when her husband nags her about not cleaning up? What does the husband feel when his wife makes excuses ("I'm too tired, I have a migraine")? What does the wife feel when she cannot overcome her resentment about her husband's nagging and refuses his romantic advances?

Each partner writes his and her feelings, for no longer than ten minutes. State only how you *feel* about your partner's behavior. Use adjectives—"angry," "disappointed," "frustrated." And don't shy away from colorful descriptions of how you really feel—"It makes me climb a wall" or "I could grab you by the shoulders and shake you." Stay away from judgments. The words "I feel" are often misused to express a judgment—"I feel you're not honest with me." Whenever you can, substitute "I think" for "I feel," what has been expressed is a judgment. True feelings are expressed by saying "I am . . ." You cannot say "I think angry," only "I am angry."

Feelings are spontaneous. They are neither good nor bad. But they can be positive or negative. Don't hesitate to share your negative feelings, but avoid "garbage dumping." Don't try to justify your feelings, just acknowledge their existence. Every time you say "I feel . . . because," you are indicating that you have not accepted your feelings. You are trying to prove and justify them. Accepting your feelings does not mean you have no control over actions that spring from them. Actions can be harmful or helpful to yourself and to others. When you face an emotion honestly, that may open new ways of dealing with it. A frank dialogue with your partner will help. A *WEDS* dialogue between partners is guided by these rules:

- Stay with feelings. This avoids unnecessary arguments. If the wife says, "If you leave your socks on the floor, I get furious," the husband cannot argue about that and say, "No, it does *not* make you furious."

- Avoid counter-accusations. Don't say: "Well, what about you? *You* leave the unwashed dishes in the sink."

- Avoid letting the dialogue spread beyond the problem at hand, or dragging in past events: "Last week you did this . . . Last month you did that . . . When your mother visits, you are especially picky. And she's the one who makes the greatest mess."

- Avoid personal attacks. Not: "Messpots like you make me furious," but "When anyone leaves things around I get furious." Describe your anger as vividly as you can and if possible with humor.

- Deal with one problem at a time. The unwashed dishes and mother's visits can be discussed in later dialogues.

- Discuss alternative actions. After openly expressing and acknowledging your emotions, you can discuss actions that are possible in spite of the feelings you each have.

Self-Help Dialogue

The WAMFA game includes a self-help dialogue. Fruitful questions in a husband-wife dialogue should stress the positive. These might include:

- What first attracted you to me?
- Which of your qualities made me want to marry you?
- Which of your qualities do I like today?
- What do we have in common?
- Where don't we understand each other fully? What can we do about understanding each other more fully?
- How do you feel when I am not open to you and not listening to you?
- How do you feel when I really listen and hear you?
- Describe your feelings in three instances when you felt close to me.
- How do you feel when I fail to show confidence in you?
- How do you feel when I do show confidence in you?
- What are your feelings about your commitment to me? My commitment to you? Our sexual relations? Our communication with each other?
- What are your feelings about me right now? (This question can be handled as letters you exchange with your spouse, and which you mail a week after you write them, to rekindle feelings aroused by the dialogue.)

Meaning in Family Relationships

Elisabeth Lukas defines a healthy family as one in which every member has a meaningful function. Such a family has neither functional gaps nor functional collisions. Like life itself, the family places demands on each member that must be fulfilled if family relationships are to be meaningful.

A young mother, for instance, has a relatively large function regarding her infants and small children. If she seeks self-actualization in a career or social activities, a functional gap may develop. That gap could be filled by another person, such as a grandmother who lives with the family. As the children grow up, the mother's function diminishes. If she continues to play the protective role of earlier years and treats her children as if they are still babies, a function collision will occur.

In a healthy family, each member is aware of her or his function in the family, even though these functions change over time. Awareness of one's functions is especially critical in times of stress (unemployment, sickness, a new child, aging, death) that may require some family members to take on additional responsibilities or give up some benefits. A healthy family needs to be alert to two situations that jeopardize its well being:

1. Does one member give orders that must be carried out by the others? This can lead to functional collisions and overdemands.
2. Does each family member live her or his own life, with little concern for the others? This can lead to functional gaps, underdemands.

When family members have healthy relationships, each member of the family is aware of her or his role in the family, and each is willing to fulfill those roles within the changing situations of family life. To accomplish this awareness, each family member must mobilize two human capacities: self-distancing and self-transcendence.

Self-distancing enables you to step away from yourself (in your mind) and see where there are gaps and collisions. Without distancing, you are likely to pay attention only to your own needs and you are not likely to see the needs of others. Self-transcendence enables you, through your caring for the others in the family, to take on functions that you don't really want, or to relinquish functions that you may want to keep. Marriage and family counselors have developed numerous techniques that use logotherapeutic principles. Two that facilitate self-distancing and self-transcendence are "sculpting" and "the newspaper sheet."

Sculpting

Sculpting is self-distancing in action. The entire family pretends that they are made of clay and can be shaped at will. Each member is asked to group all family members as she or he sees them. The husband, for example, might form a group in which his wife has separated herself and stands defiantly, legs spread wide, arms crossed. He lies on the floor, helpless, while his children pull him in all directions. The wife may form a different group. She may see herself crouching while her husband stands straight with his foot on her neck; all the children but one are on her back—that one is in the corner, paying no attention to the rest of the family. The children may form various structures, each one different from the others. A child may shape the father frowning, threatening, in the posture of a bear, or isolated—perhaps not even part of the group. Mother may be hugging, preaching with lifted forefinger, or holding her hands over her ears. Brother may be shown as domineering, sister with her tongue stuck out in insolent rebellion.

Each family member has a turn being the "sculptor," and all family members must agree to follow the instructions of the "sculptor" about poses and facial expressions. The tableau will then show how each member sees the family and the relationships—pairings off, triangles, alliances, isolations, conflicts, defiances, threats, fears, and dependencies.

After each participant has "sculpted" the family members, then each is asked to form a second set of sculptures that show how each of them would *like* to see the family. After all family members have seen how they are seen by the others, and what they would like the relationships to be like, then the basic question is asked again: What would the first step be in getting from the situation as it is to the situation as it could be? Now self-transcendence is brought into play. Questions are asked about what members of the family would have to do to fill gaps, and what they would have to give up to avoid collisions. Who would be prepared, for the sake of the others, to change behavior? Sculpting might break a vicious circle that has trapped the family, so that a new beginning can be made. Sculpting can make it easier for family members to talk to each other—not only from their own perspectives, but with a measure of objectivity and even humor.

The Newspaper Sheet

This "game" also makes use of the human capacity for self-distancing. It is used to explore the relationship between two people—husband and wife, parent and child, sibling and sibling.

A sheet of newspaper big enough for two people to stand on is placed on the floor. Two people are asked to approach the sheet from oppisite directions and to stand on it. The ways they respond will give them some insight into how they "stand with each other."

The husband may strut over with self-assurance and place himself on the sheet as if to say, "It's all mine." The wife may quietly find a place in the corner. Or she may fight for her place. Or she may find her place by lovingly embracing her husband. Or by standing carefully so she won't touch him. There are numerous possibilities. And the possibilities are just as numerous for other twosomes—and just as revealing.

In the second part of the exercise, the pair is asked to step off the newspaper and to approach it again, the same way as they did the first time. But this second time they are to be conscious of their movements. They are to pay attention to every step, every hesitation, resistance, adjustment. In a subsequent Socratic dialogue, they will talk over their actions—as seen from the outside, the conscious observation of unconscious behavior. They can talk about the feelings they had while they were positioning themselves on the sheet: defiance, guilt, tenderness, triumph, weakness.

In the third part of the exercise, they place themselves on the sheet again. But this third time they assume the positions they would *like* to have in their relationship.

This exercise can be done by the pair alone, or with the rest of the family watching. If the family watches, then the others can share their observations of the pair who did the exercise. That reinforces the effect of self-distancing.

In all exercises that explore meanings in family relationships, stress the positive. Negative aspects of the relationships are not to be neglected, but observations about them should always be followed with the question: "What can we do to make things better?" Where the emotions automatically say "no," the spirit can still say "yes." Obstacles to fulfilling relationships can be removed, and new approaches are possible.

Chapter Twelve

Sharing Groups

Because the search for meaning is personal, it has been argued that the group approach is not suitable. Nevertheless, logotherapists have developed a number of successful group techniques.

When working with a group, precautions are in order. Logotherapy is based on trust between helper and seeker. This trust must be extended to all group members. "Encounter" in such groups is not aggressive but caring and positive. For this reason the term "sharing groups" is used. Each participant shares the individual search for meaning, without pressure. All must know that they always have the right to refuse to answer any question or to join in any exercise. But they also must know that their participation is welcome and will contribute to the success of the group. Everyone must be aware that whatever is said and done within the group will not be talked about beyond the group.

The search for meaning must remain personal, and care must be taken to avoid peer pressures within the group. The Socratic dialogue becomes a "multilogue." The helper must assure that participants do not try to solve problems for each other. The discovery of meaning remains the responsibility of the individual. Suggestions are welcome, but not in the form of advice that prompts a "yes but" reaction. The experiences of group members are most effective when presented as examples, especially after a logohint has emerged. Participants may say, "Yes, I was once in the same situation and I did such-and-such." The decision is left to the seeker; the other group members have simply helped the seeker to see alternatives.

General Guidelines

Robert Leslie and other logotherapists have outlined some guidelines for sharing groups:

- Create a supportive atmosphere in which communication in its freest, most uninhibited, most personal sense can take place.
- Make participants aware of the resources of the human spirit: self-discovery, choice, uniqueness, responsibility, and self-transcendence.
- Help them see that it is in their power to use these resources to find meaning directions.
- Help them find out where they are, where they want to go, and how to get there, step by step.
- Focus attention on what's right with them, and how they can learn from what they think is wrong with them.

Responsibilities for Group Members

Each member accepts responsibility for the life of the group. Each participates and interacts, without waiting for the helper to straighten out difficulties.

Communication is sought on a deeper level than is usual in social relationships. Stay on a personal level. When talking about books, movies, or the experiences of other people, state how *you* feel about these.

Make the present situation the focus of your attention, but without ignoring the past. Don't use the past as explanation or excuse for present failures. Instead, learn from both the mistakes and the achievements of the past.

The emphasis in the group is on personal sharing, rather than on diagnostic probing. Stay in the area in which you are the world's greatest expert: Your feelings and experiences.

Observations are welcome, but attacks are discouraged. Instead of saying, "You have a very annoying way of interrupting me," say "I feel annoyed whenever I am interrupted."

Responsibilities for Helpers

The characteristics most important in helpers are empathy, warmth, gentleness, genuineness, and willingness not to talk too much. Helpers have eight main functions:

1. Structuring: Starting and ending at the appointed time, providing support for the contributions of each person, protecting members from destructive attacks.

2. Mirroring: Making observations about what is happening, observing incongruities between words and actions, pointing out behavior patterns.

3. Focusing: Helping the group move from social chitchat into dialogue with greater depth, from impersonal, peripheral issues to personal involvement with significant concerns.

4. Modeling: Actively participating as one of the group, according to the rules agreed upon.

5. Nudging: Encouraging participants toward change. "Where do you go from here?" "What are you going to do about it?"

6. Linking: Tying together disconnected statements, picking up unfinished business.

7. Sharing: Participating in group discussions and allowing members to participate in helping other group members.

8. Policing: Seeing to it that the group is not disrupted by the behavior of individual members.

Note: In a group that is working well, the functions of the helper are shared by the participants. The participants may be as important as the helper.

Examples

Fred, a young man, hardly took part in the group. Several times during each session, he left the room and then returned after a few minutes. Eventually one of the members of the group became irritated and asked Fred, "Why do you come here at all? You never say anything and you constantly disturb us by going in and out." Others in the group attacked Fred for his behavior, and before the helper intervened the following dialogue took place:

> *Fred:* I have a German shepherd in my car, and I have to go out every so often to see if he's all right.
> *Group member:* You disturb the group just for a dog?
> *Fred:* He's lonely.
> *Group member:* Is he more important to you than we are?
> *Fred:* I love my dog.

The way Fred said that captured the group's attention. That was the first time Fred had shown any emotion. In the discussion that followed, a woman in the group told Fred that she and her husband also had a dog they loved. She said that they hated to put their dog in a kennel when they went on a trip, because the dog evidently was unhappy there. They were planning to go away for the weekend—would Fred consider taking care of their dog? The woman said that, because Fred loved animals, he would give her dog more personal attention than he got at the kennel. She said she and her husband would gladly pay Fred the same amount they would have to pay to the kennel. Fred was flabbergasted by the proposal and, after a little prodding, he accepted. During conversations at subsequent meetings of the group, it became evident that that was the first time in his life that anyone had offered to pay Fred for something he actually enjoyed doing.

From that day on, Fred's participation in the group increased, and the other members accepted him as one of their own. At the last session all of the members of the group were asked to give their impressions of each other. One of the participants said to Fred: "When I first saw you, I thought you were a bum. But now I know you are a good person. You love animals. I hope that one day you'll find a person, maybe a young woman, you will learn to love."

Fred gave the group a number of logohints. He was asked to make a list of activities that could be meaningful for him. It was not surprising that animals were important in the activities he listed. Fred selected one item from that list of alternatives: he decided to become a volunteer at an animal hospital. As the first step toward this goal, Fred placed an ad in a newspaper and found an unpaid job cleaning up in a pet shop. He returned to high school, graduated, and was hired by the pet shop to care for the animals. Later he found a job at an animal hospital and started junior college, with the hope that he would eventually become a veterinarian. At about that time he moved in with his girl friend. This drift toward a happy ending had started with an uncomfortable incident in a sharing group.

In a sharing group, an embarrassing incident that would be hushed over in a social setting can become a first step toward real understanding. Robert Leslie reports that, in one group, a young woman arrived late and apologized by saying that she had felt sick because she was pregnant. "What's worse, I didn't want to become pregnant while my husband is still in school."

Another woman in the group exploded. "What's the matter with you?" she shouted. "How stupid can you be? Haven't you ever heard of birth control?"

There was an embarrassed silence. In a social setting, someone would have quickly changed the subject. But this was not a social group, it was a sharing group. The helper asked the group, "How did you feel when Sue (the attacker) spoke to Polly (the pregnant wife)?" Many in the group expressed anger at Sue for the sharpness of her attack. The helper let the discussion go on for a while, then asked: "Now, how do you think Sue feels?"

Sue spoke up, telling the group how she felt. "I've wanted to get pregnant for years, but for some reason I can't."

Suddenly the mood of the group changed. Instead of dealing with an angry attack, they realized that they had been hearing the anguish of a young woman's suffering—expressed awkwardly and communicated poorly, but real nevertheless. The participants learned a good deal from this simple incident.

The Opening Session

In a group, shared trust and positive attitudes must be cultivated from the beginning. The participants sit in a circle, on comfortable chairs or cushions. They are probably all a bit anxious, and a relaxed helper sets an example. A little humor helps, too. The participants are asked to say a few words about themselves, about what they hope to gain from the group experience, and about something positive in their present lives. The helper participates in this introductory exercise, and in all the group activities.

These introductory moments can be dramatized and enlivened, if that seems appropriate. The helper and the participants can form a circle, while everyone is still standing. The helper, holding a ball of wool, introduces herself or himself, says something positive, and then—holding onto the end of the yarn—throws the ball of wool across the circle to one of the participants.

The person who catches the ball repeats what the helper has just said: "You are Fred Jones, a high school teacher, and you are happy because you have just become a father." Then he introduces himself, mentions something positive about himself and, holding the string in his hands, throws the ball to another person in the circle. This pattern is repeated again and again, until everyone in the circle has participated. The ball of wool gets smaller as a network is established that links the participants.

Each person repeats what the previous one has said. This "game" demonstrates their interdependence, and motivates them to listen carefully to what the others are saying.

Then the sequence is reversed. The last person to receive the ball throws it back to the person who threw it to him or her, trying to remember what that person had said. Again the pattern is repeated by each person in the circle. The network disappears, the ball becomes larger, everyone has learned something about all the others, and everyone in the group is relaxed and having fun.

If the participants seem shy and nervous and say little or nothing (which they have the right to do) during the introduction, the first session can be started in a different way: Each person can be asked to select a partner (a stranger rather than a friend), and the diads are asked to talk to each other for twenty minutes.

For the first ten minutes A listens to B, and for the other ten minutes B listens to A. Then everyone joins in one circle and tells what they have heard in the diads. A tells what B said, and B is asked if anything needs to be corrected or added. Then B tells what A said, and A is given a chance to correct or add. This gives the group information they probably would not have gotten if all the participants had spoken directly to the group. This also serves as an exercise in listening, which is important in groups.

During the first session participants do not go much below the surface. But communication is begun.

The Group Process

The ideas that form the basis of the logotherapeutic approach should not be presented to the group in lectures. Instead those ideas should be fed gradually, in small helpings, when they seem appropriate. The basic information can come from books that the group members read. All of the ideas, exercises, games, and techniques that have been discussed in this book can be adapted to the group process.

List Making

People in groups can achieve self-distancing. As a participant shares an experience with the others in the group, he sees himself through the eyes of others. An introductory list-making exercise can facilitate this process.

Ask participants to make two lists: what they like about themselves, and what they dislike about themselves. The self-discovery that results from this list making is enhanced by the comments of the other group members. Even people who sit quietly during discussion are likely to have "aha" insights into themselves.

"Aha, that's the way I feel, too" they will say in expressing surprised self-discovery in response to the remark of another member of the group. Open discussion of everyone's lists widens the alternatives. One person may say "That's a possibility I never thought of" in reaction to someone else's list. Another person may say "Hey, I'm not the only one who procrastinates," cheered to realize how often procrastination turns up on the "dislike" lists. The sharing of likes and dislikes can be comforting.

The helper must see to it that the "multilogue" of the group does not deteriorate into a sharing of despair. This does not mean that problems are neglected, but instead that attention is focused on solutions. Humor is always helpful. One woman, after listening to the long list of things another group member did not like about himself, quoted an Austrian comedy writer: "No one is completely worthless. One can always serve as a horrible example."

The helper tries to keep all participants involved. This requires sensitivity. Is the quiet person shy and in need of encouragement, or should she be left alone? The helper must exercise tactful judgment. One member of the group talks a great deal. Does that individual need to be restrained from dominating the discussion, or does that person have an intense problem that needs to be heard?

In any event, it is unwise to focus too much attention on one member. That person may begin to feel uncomfortable, and the others may feel neglected. When a member has a serious problem, a private appointment between seeker and helper can be arranged. Or the whole group can be more directly included in working with the problem.

Logodrama

One way to involve the group in a problem presented by one member is to involve the members in a logodrama. Logodrama can give you an opportunity to play out your problem situation by taking on the parts of various people with whom you have conflicts (partner, parent, sibling, boss).

When you use logodrama in a group, you do not need an empty chair. The individual with the problem plays himself or herself and becomes the "director" of a logodrama in which members of the group are cast in the various other parts—wife, lover, teen-age daughter, mother-in-law. The director outlines the situation and the problem and gives instructions to the other players about the characters they are to play.

If the behavior of one of the actors is unlike that of the character he is portraying, the director stops the play and gives additional directions. Group members who are not in the "cast" serve as observers and can participate by "doubling": If a group member thinks of something that one of the characters might say, the doubler walks behind the person portraying that character, places a hand on that person's shoulder, and says what he thinks that person might say. The person portraying the character can then repeat the doubler's suggested line.

For example: Jack has a problem with his brother, who causes trouble and then carefully maneuvers the situation so that Jack is blamed.

> *Jack* (to the person who is playing his brother): You, uh, really shouldn't have done this. Mom got mad at me, and I, uh well, I couldn't prove anything. It wasn't my fault, but Mom got mad at me.
>
> *Group member* (stepping behind Jack, placing his hand on Jack's shoulder, and shouting at Jack's "brother"): You goddamned liar. All of my life you've gotten me into hot water!
>
> *Jack* (shouting): You goddamned liar. You hypocrite. All of my life you have gotten me into hot water!!

In the discussion that followed, the group member who had done the doubling explained that he felt that Jack's problem was that he did not know how to express his anger. Jack agreed. If he had not agreed, he would have told the doubler that he could not accept the words the doubler had spoken. Doubling can help people see that they cannot express love, that they wear masks over their true personalities (by playing the clown, the good-natured patsy, the sexpot, the macho man). Doubling can open the door to new insights.

Example

Verna was in a sharing group of high school dropouts. She lived with her parents on their farm, was very active in the local 4-H club, and was an A student. Then her mother died in an accident. Verna took over her mother's chores on the farm, in addition to her school and club activities.

Soon she was exhausted. She dropped out of school and left the 4-H club. Verna's aunt—her mother's sister—wanted Verna to come to live with her in the city. Verna and the group members enacted a logodrama about this situation.

> *"Aunt":* Come and live with me. You are young and have to lead a normal life for a 17-year-old. Even if you don't love me, don't you love yourself?
>
> *Verna:* I do love you. But Father needs me. (To the member playing Verna's father): I want to stay on the farm. I really do.
>
> *"Aunt":* You say you are too tired to have a date, even to go to a movie. 4-H stands for head, heart, hands, and health. All you use is your hands. You are ruining your health.
>
> *"Father":* It's only for a while, until I have paid off my debts.
>
> *Verna:* Dad, I'm keeping your books. We'll be in trouble for a long time.
>
> *Member of the group doubling for Verna:* Dad, you are an irresponsible, selfish man.
>
> *Verna* (to the doubler): No, I wouldn't say that.
>
> *Doubler:* Well, what would you say?
>
> *Verna:* Maybe he *should* take more responsibility. But he's not selfish. He loves me and I love him.
>
> *Helper:* Say that to your father.
>
> *Verna* (after a long hesitation): Dad, I want to stay with you. I love you. I don't mind the work. But ... I do miss school, and my friends, and a little fun once in a while. I don't want to live in the city, but Aunt Hilde is right ... well, half right. I am using my head and my hands. But my heart hurts and my health isn't good. Sometimes I have to take pep pills to stay awake to fix dinner.
>
> *Doubler:* Dad, you have to relieve me of some responsibility. I want to work, but I also want to have dates, go to movies.
>
> *Verna:* Dad, you have to relieve me of some responsibility. We'll have to work this out.

The problem has not been solved—that is not what sharing groups are for. But doors have been opened.

Feedback Effect

In sharing groups, the feedback effect can provide additional benefits when used with any exercise described in this book, including logodramas.

When seekers draw life maps that show ups and downs, turning points, relationships, bright and dark areas, they can take turns pinning their maps on the wall and discussing them. Feedback from group members about life maps can open new vistas.

A career woman who had drawn a life map was taken aback by the question, "Where is your family in this picture?" Another group member was cheered by the comment, "I'm glad to see that in every clump of black and brown there is a spot of green—it is as if you see new life sprouting from every hopeless situation." A man in the group who complained about the chaos in his life was told: "Look at the blue lines in all that hodgepodge—those lines form a star pattern." Another man was startled by the observation: "Funny that you used the same orange color to draw your divorce—which you said was the worst thing that happened to you—and finding your church—which you said was the best. What do they have in common?" After a moment's reflection the man replied, "I guess they both made me grow."

The "as if" game (see Appendix B) also can take on additional dimensions through feedback from a group. In a safe group environment among trusted people, a wallflower can behave like the sensual woman she feels she is, and can hear the reactions and the constructive criticism of the other group members.

Feedback can be used in many ways. One man in a group believed that he never had anything to say that was worth listening to. He was asked to sit in the center of the circle and to demand attention for every word he said. A woman in the group had been brought up to believe that self-praise is arrogant and impolite. She was asked to sit in the center of the circle and to loudly proclaim all of her own good points, while other members of the group called out additional positive features they believed were hidden in her. A "recorder" made written notes of all the qualities that were mentioned. The woman took the list home to think about.

Meaning Through Books

Robert Leslie and other logotherapists use books in groups as guideposts to meaning. The readings are used, not for intellectual discussions, but as springboards for personal insights. The story of Job can lead to personal explorations: "How do I deal with undeserved suffering?" The story of Joseph and his brothers evokes contemplation about problems with siblings. The story of Adam and Eve can lead to reflection about what it means to say "no" to authority, even to God, and what it means to face the consequences.

Leslie, in his book *Jesus as Counselor*, explores eleven stories from the Scriptures that can be the basis for group discussions. These include the story of Zacchaeus, Luke 19:1-10 (mobilizing the defiant power); the parable of the rich young ruler, Mark 10:17-22 (finding a personal life task); and the tale of the paralyzed youth, Mark 2:2-12 (resolving value conflicts).

Leslie also uses modern literature for discussing personal issues: Thornton Wilder's *Our Town* to explore personal relationships; Alice Walker's *The Color Purple* to validate the finding of meaning in impossible circumstances by rising above them; Arthur Miller's *All My Sons* and *Death of a Salesman* to think about one's own father-son relationships; or John Steinbeck's *East of Eden* to allow group participants to talk about their choice-making after an unfortunate choice has become irreversible.

Dereflection Groups

Dr. Lukas "graduates" clients from individual counseling through dereflection groups. When former clients return to the stresses of regular living, the positive outlook that each has developed in counseling needs to be fortified.

The dereflection group has one rule that distinguishes it from other sharing groups where the emphasis is on problems. In dereflection groups, only positive aspects of each person's life may be discussed. If a participant dwells on the negative, the group points out that that is in violation of the basic rule of the group. If the negative individual has an unresolved problem that still needs work, the helper will arrange a private session.

Most people pay more attention to minor troubles than to pleasant experiences. They expect difficulties and notice them. In dereflection groups, attention is directed toward positive incidents, even minor ones—someone smiling at you, a bird singing, a beautiful cloud pattern. Each group participant is asked to keep a diary of pleasant experiences and encounters, and to look at their daily entries every night before going to bed. In the group, each participant is asked to relate three positive incidents experienced or observed since the previous meeting. The affirmative is made the center of attention.

A dereflection group also uses positive (meaningful) associations. After a short relaxation exercise, participants are asked to sit quietly, with eyes closed. The helper mentions, at intervals, words or phrases such as "evening" or "summer" or "playing with children." Group members are asked to quietly associate these words with whatever comes to mind. Then these associations are discussed in the group.

Lukas has found that what a participant may consider positive and meaningful may not at first seem, to an objective observer, to be positive. She cites as an example one woman's response to the phrase "last summer." The woman had made a pleasurable trip to Greece the previous summer. But when "last summer" was mentioned she thought, instead, of a dead cat. In explanation she told the group a story:

During the previous summer, she had a fight on the phone with her boyfriend. Afterward she decided to walk over to his house to "really let him have it." On the way over, she saw a dead cat in the street. That made her think about how short life is, and she realized that she did not want to waste precious moments fighting over trivialities. When she reached her boyfriend's home, she was in a different mood from the one in which she had left home. Instead of fighting again and separating, they reconciled and made up. This was the episode that came to her mind first when she thought of "last summer."

Meditation Groups

This type of group is also used by Lukas as "graduation" from individual therapy. And it has general applications. A meditation group uses stories and parables that stimulate meditative discussions. These may come from logotherapeutic literature, world literature, the Scriptures, fairy tales, or mythology. Frankl uses many metaphors and similes that lend themselves to such meditative exercises (some have already been mentioned in this book).

- The wall calendar from which you tear off a sheet each day is described in Chapter Seven. You can observe sadly that each day fewer and fewer sheets, and days, remain. Or you can note, happily, that the growing pile of torn-off sheets represents events that you have experienced and that no one can take from you.
- The infant who suffers the pain of an injection has no way of knowing that the injection will protect him from a disease.
- The unique qualities of an airplane are revealed only after the plane has taken off—just as an individual's specifically human qualities become most evident after that person has "taken off" into the dimension of the spirit.
- The Bible is full of stories that lend themselves to meditative discussions—from Jacob's struggle with the angel to the parable of the Prodigal Son.
- Secular literature abounds with suitable stories, from Faust's search for meaning to Hamlet's search for justice and Don Quixote's search for love.
- Every fairy tale and mythological story, from "The Ugly Duckling" to "Sisyphus" can serve as a basis for meditative group discussion.

Concluding Exercises

All sharing groups should end on a hopeful and positive note, so that participants will return to their lives strengthened and will continue to think about the search for meaning. Self-confidence will have been reinforced. At the last session of the group, members can participate in an exercise that emphasizes the positive aspects of the shared experience of searching for meaning.

In one exercise, the group sits in a circle and each members says something about everyone else. After so many sessions together, it is hardly necessary to stress that comments should be upbeat. Some criticism can be useful, if it is communicated in a way that shows clearly that it is meant to be constructive.

In another exercise, each participant is given as many slips of paper as there are other members in the group. Each person is asked to write something positive about each of the other participants. The slips are folded, with the name of the subject of the comment on the outside. The helper collects the slips and then redistributes them to the people to whom they are addressed. Each group member receives a collection of positive statements to be kept.

When the last meeting ends, group members stand in a circle, arms around each others shoulders, and have a last chance as a group to express their feelings—about what they have learned, and about what they take home with them. In a sharing group that has been led well, friendships are almost always formed that continue after the group ends.

Appendix A

Finding Meaning Every Day

A sharing group provides the members with tools for restructuring their lives in ways that are meaningful to them, so that their daily behavior more nearly expresses their values. Plans for eight sessions of a sharing group focus on these topics:

1. Introduction to Logotherapy
2. Your Value Hierarchy
3. Handling Tension
4. Meaningful Changes in Daily Activities
5. How To Deal with Crises
6. How To Deal with Meaninglessness
7. How To Deal with Depression
8. What You Have Learned for Daily Living

One of the basic assumptions of logotherapy is that deep within your spiritual unconscious you know what kind of person you are and can become; what direction you want to go; and what behavior is meaningful to you. Superimposed on this innate knowledge is the self you project to assure self-preservation and acceptance. Whenever these two "selves" conflict, you feel at odds with yourself.

Adapted from an article by John M. Quirk, Vancouver, British Columbia, published in *The International Forum for Logotherapy*, 2(2), 1979.

When you want to make changes toward meaning, you're likely to talk in general terms—about wanting to be "more caring" or "more assertive," or to "procrastinate less." These are goals, and it is important to have goals. But changes will occur only when you take actual steps toward your goals.

If you want to be more caring, you have to ask yourself, "During the past week, what did I do that expressed caring, and can I do more of the same?" Or, "Which of my actions during the past week expressed noncaring, and what can I do to prevent that kind of behavior?"

Example: Mrs. B, a woman who was shy and had problems in her marriage, said she wanted to be more affectionate, a better wife, and a better mother. As long as she continued to belabor herself with such statements, she was not likely to make any real changes. When I asked her to be more specific, she said she wanted to be more understanding of her husband and closer to her children. That was still not specific enough, so I asked her: "What have you done during the past month that illustrates that you are *not* the kind of wife you want to be, *not* the mother you want to be, and—most important of all—not the kind of person you want to be?"

I suggested to Mrs. B that she write in her journal every week, and that she begin each entry with a sentence that started: "I was not affectionate this week when . . . " and include several specific examples. At our fourth group meeting Mrs. B said she had compiled a list of behaviors that she could improve in the direction of meaning as she saw it.

For instance, her husband often came home at 1 A.M. He was an architect and did a lot of drafting at night. He would come home and go into the kitchen for the sandwich that she had prepared and left for him in the refrigerator. Then he would go into the bedroom, turn on the television set, and watch for about fifteen minutes while he got ready for bed. Mrs. B said that this "drove me up a wall."

The group did some brainstorming about what could be done to break this nightly ritual. Every woman in the group speculated about what she would do in the same situation.

"If he were my husband," one woman said, "I would get out of bed and sit next to him and watch the program with him, until he was relaxed enough to go to bed."

Mrs. B thought that was a meaningless activity, but she agreed to try it three times. When she returned to the group the following week, she was a transformed woman. She had done as the group member had suggested. And she had also done something as a mother—three times during the past week she had hugged her two boys before they left for school. She had now experienced two different behavior patterns, and she said, "I was really affectionate last week." Looking at her, we could see evidence of a change.

These were small events, but they really made a difference to Mrs. B, and enabled her to see that she was capable of being "more affectionate." From that time on she was able to build into her life a structure of different behaviors that enabled her to achieve more meaningful relationships.

This process could not have started with generalities. If Mrs. B had started by speculating about what a meaningful relationship between a wife and husband would be like, she would have come up with ideas like "We should have more time together" or "We ought to think of each other as the most important person in the world." And she would have contrasted these ideals with her own miserable situation. That would probably have led to feelings of greater inadequacy and to inability to act to change her life.

Attention to specifics is given throughout all eight sessions.

First Session: Introduction to Logotherapy

After the introduction the helper tells the group what they are going to do together. On the blackboard are listed the topics for the eight weeks the group is to meet. The group will introduce themselves soon, but first the helper wants to find out how everyone is feeling. The helper asks the group members to rate themselves on a scale from 1 to 5 (5 signifies feeling very good and 1 signifies feeling depressed) and to indicate the direction in which they are moving.

This is done at the beginning of each session, all participants state how they are and which way they are going. For example, people say "I'm at 3 and holding" or "I'm at 2 and going up" or "I'm at 5 and really high, and I have to watch myself so that any downturn will not be too steep." Someone who is depressed may not want to say any more than "I'm at 1 and hanging in there."

These self-ratings enable the helper to fashion each session according to the needs of the group. If most members are at 1 or 2, the helper is likely to concentrate on the problems that are currently bothering them. When most members are at or near 5, the helper can take a more intellectual approach and talk about logotherapy—when people are feeling good, it is easier for them to understand and accept the principles of logotherapy and apply those to their own situations.

The first twenty minutes of such a session can be spent discussing the basic concepts of logotherapy, stressing three dimensions of the individual—the somatic (physical), the psychological, and the noetic (spiritual). It is important that the participants understand the concept of the noetic dimension and the area of the essential self. You *have* a body and a psyche, but you *are* your *noos* (spirit). It is also important to stress that the human spirit is not reserved for people with religious inclinations but is a human dimension that is part of everyone. You cannot understand humans in their fullness unless you see them in their three-dimensional totality.

The first exercise that the helper does with the group helps the participants to distinguish the three dimensions. Group members are asked to list in their notebooks moments when they felt fulfilled, and to indicate whether the meaning of that fulfillment originated in the somatic, psychological, or noetic dimension. People write statements like these:

My life has meaning when I jog (somatic)
"   receive praise (psychological)
"   am with my grandchildren (noetic)
"   do pottery (noetic)
"   play bridge (psychological)
"   have a good meal (somatic)
"   am with friends (noetic)

This exercise forces people to think about the differences between the dimensions, and to learn to distinguish among them. It is important for people to know where their fulfillment originates. Making love, for instance, can be meaningful in all three dimensions. People have some difficulty differentiating between the psychological and the noetic dimensions. Here is a guide for making this distinction:

Psychological	Noetic
We do things because we are driven.	We are the drivers; we make decisions, take responsibility, accept commitments.
We respond to a "need."	We express a personal choice.
Motivation is pleasure, power, prestige.	Motivation is meaning.
We act for self-actualization.	We act for self-transcendence; we act for the sake of someone or something.

After this exercise, it is time for the group members to briefly introduce themselves. Until now they have been thinking in general terms about what is meaningful in their lives. The rest of this session is taken up with specifics. Group members are asked to write in their notebooks answers to these questions:

- What happened last week that made my life meaningful in each of the three areas?
- What happened last week that made my life meaningless in each of the three areas?

The participants form small groups of three or four. Each of these groups discusses the statements that the participants decide to share. Note: Logogroups function with one general rule—everyone can at any time refuse to reveal information or answer questions, but answers given and information shared are to be as honest as possible.

Homework

In preparation for the second session, participants are asked to do homework:

1. Draw a map of your life, from the beginning to the present, with its ups and downs and main events. Extend your map into the future. No drawing skill is desired or expected. Don't pay attention to how well you draw, but let forms, shapes, symbols, and colors flow from your noetic unconscious. Don't plan ahead. Let things happen. Use a large sheet of paper and colored pens or crayons.
2. Answer these three questions:
   Who do I think I am?
   Who does my family want me to be?
   Who do I want to be?

Second Session: Your Value Hierarchy

Members bring to the session the maps they have made as homework. Again the participants form small groups of three or four, and they discuss the maps. The exercise of making the maps and the group discussions help group members to be aware of where they come from, of the influences that are present in their value hierarchies, of the meanings of past events that they now see with a new perspective.

The significance of an event that once seemed very meaningful may have changed, faded. Or an event that did not seem significant when it occurred may now, in retrospect, seem relevant. Participants are encouraged to keep adding to their drawings during this and subsequent sessions, as they have new insights. And they are reminded to pay attention to the colors, symbols, and other ways they use as they become aware of messages from the unconscious.

One woman drew her graduation from college (which she had marked as a happy event) with the same color she used for her subsequent divorce (which had plunged her into great misery). Now, eight years later, when she saw that, she realized that her noetic unconscious recognized in the meaning of her divorce an element shared with the meaning of her graduation—a maturing toward independence.

After the group members have discussed their road maps, they are asked to write the following questions, and answers to them, in their notebooks:

- What values have I learned from my family?
- List three ways in which I am like my father.
- List three ways in which I am like my mother.
- List three ways in which I am different from my father.
- List three ways in which I am different from my mother.

- List three behaviors in the past week when I was like my father.
- List three behaviors in the past week when I was like my mother.
- List three behaviors in the past week when I was different from my father.
- List three behaviors in the past week when I was different from my mother.

Now the helper talks briefly about Frankl's distinction between meanings and values as guides to daily behavior. Underlying this talk is the basic tenet of logotherapy that life offers you meanings in every moment and every situation. To recognize the "meaning of the moment" and to respond to it is to lead a meaningful life. The individual who takes on this responsibility—response-ability—to the demands of the moment often must make difficult choices.

In this choice-making you are helped by your values—by what generations of people have found meaningful in similar situations in the past. When you rely on the values of others, you are spared the personal search for meaning. But conflicts can result when a situation evokes conflicting values.

As an exercise, the group is asked to write down examples of value conflicts that they have experienced and examples of situations in which they took a stand against accepted values. During this second session, the helper encourages the participants to find out, by looking at their road maps, where their values come from, how strong their values are, and what changes they want to make. Participants are encouraged to develop and record their own personal hierarchies of values. The helper can ask the group members to call out the values they consider important. These are listed on the blackboard and can be used by group members as they make their hierarchical lists of values.

Homework

Draw a pie of your daily activities, to show how much time you spend, in an average day, on various activities.

Write two statements:

- The best day of the week is ...
- The worst day of the week is ...

Use the Social Readjustment Rating Scale (in Appendix H) to evaluate your current tension. And complete the PIL and SONG tests (Appendices F and G respectively). [The helper has made copies of this material and distributes these to group members.]

Third Session: Handling Tension

Participants are asked to reevaluate their road maps and to add to them if they wish. Where were the meaningful and the meaningless points? Where were the turning points? It is common to find a turning point during a period of stress. The group then talks about turning points.

Frankl's stress theory, which distinguishes between physical-psychological tension and noetic stress, is now discussed by the helper. Physical-psychological tension is unhealthy and needs to be overcome or adjusted to. Noetic stress brings a healthy tension that is part of growth and the search for meaning. It must not be adjusted to or tranquilized away. Frankl defines noetic stress as tension between what you are and what you want to become—your outreach toward what you are "meant to be."

Group members look at the Social Readjustment Rating Scale, which measures the physical-psychological tensions. It is important to realize that tensions caused by happy events are as stress producing as are tensions caused by unhappy events. The stress of marrying is only 15 points lower than the stress of marital separation. Even apparently neutral changes—say, in financial status—produce stress, whether the change is for better or worse.

Participants are encouraged to fill out the Social Readjustment Rating Scale once a month for at least a year. Some stresses can be controlled. Awareness of such stresses can help you to avoid additional tensions. For instance, it is usually not wise, after a death in the family, to get a divorce or change your job or residence. It is best for most people to avoid stresses that total more than 150 points on the scale. If you fill out the scale each month, when you realize that you are going through a period of mounting tension, you can plan what to put off, and when.

To determine tension in the noetic dimension, a comparison between the PIL (Purpose in Life) and the SONG (Seeking of Noetic Goals) tests is useful. These tests have been worked out by the logotherapist James C. Crumbaugh and are available from The Institute of Logotherapy, P. O. Box 2852, Saratoga, California 95070. (Test plus manual, $4.00; 25 copies of test without manual, $4.75.)

The PIL test measures the degree to which you have found meaning and purpose in life. The SONG test measures the strength of your motivation to find meaning. These two tests also should be taken once a month for at least one year.

Combined use of the two tests reveals the tension between your meaning orientation (PIL) and the strength of your motivation to find it (SONG). Those who score low on PIL and high on SONG can profit from logotherapy, because they lack meaning and are motivated to find it. Those who score low on SONG need to be motivated to use the will to meaning.

Again in groups of three or four, participants discuss how they can reduce their current physical-psychological stresses, or at least make those manageable, and how they can sustain the motivation to continue the healthy stress of a search for meaning. Participants are asked to write in their notebooks examples of experiences during the previous week when they were motivated to:

- make a meaningful choice
- make a responsible decision
- take on a self-chosen task
- respond to the demands of the moment
- do something for a person or a cause

Homework

List five behaviors that are meaningful to you.
List five behaviors that are meaningless to you.
List ten things you *have* to do in the next month.
List ten things you *want* to do in the next month.
Revise your pie of daily activities, if necessary.

Fourth Session: Meaningful Changes in Daily Activities

Group members are now ready to talk about practical, meaningful behavior changes in their daily activities, quite apart from all theories. At the start of this session, the helper asks the participants to write down their long-range goals for the next five years. About twenty minutes is scheduled for this exercise.

Then each member of the group puts together a package that contains the most recent homework—the five behaviors that are most meaningful, the five that are least meaningful, the ten things he or she must do in the next month, and the ten that he or she wants to do in the next month. Each person adds a list of long-range goals. Then each person marks his or her package with a symbol and drops it into a basket.

The next step is for each group member to pick one of those packages from the basket. Then each person has the entire framework for daily behavior of another person: a statement of goals, what is meaningful and meaningless, a list of things that need to be done, a list of desired activities, and the daily activities. After everyone has read the material in the package selected from the basket, each is asked to act as "consultant"—to write down a plan for how the unknown "client" might structure his or her life for the next month, or even the next six months, to approach his or her goals.

This exercise is useful for both the consultants and the clients. The consultants have enough distance to see what practical changes can be suggested—changes that they would be unable to suggest for themselves or for someone close. And the clients hear suggestions for choices in daily behavior that they might not have thought of alone. During this exercise, it is clear to all that these choices and changes are merely suggestions, and that it is up to the client to decide which ones to accept and act on. Traps are sprung, doors are opened, and new choices are made visible.

Next, each participant—by means of the symbol on the package chosen from the basket—matches the package with the person who created it, the person whose materials he or she has read and for whom he or she has written a suggested new life structure. Often the consultants are amazed, even scared, to see whose life they have restructured.

During my first participation in this session, a shy woman selected my material. It was evident that if I had asked her, directly, to make suggestions for my life, she would have felt totally helpless. Yet what she wrote I found to be extremely useful. And when she realized how useful her suggestions were, her self-image was changed in ways that were helpful to her.

The consultant and the clients discuss the suggested behavior changes. The clients decide which of the suggestions are practical and what adjustments could be made. Then the clients write down their version of meaningful new behavior—for the next month and the next year. The group members take home their adapted version of the consultant's suggestions, to use as a basis for assessing how close they have come to realizing their own proposals. Group members are encouraged to write in their journals/notebooks, perhaps once a month, a statement that starts: "I am nearer to my goals because . . ." The first of these reevaluations can be done before the eight-week workshop ends.

It is, of course, desirable to keep your structure flexible, and to constantly revise it in practical—not philosophical—terms. It is important that your structure is your own, based on your statements of meanings, values, and priorities. You need a flexible structure because, although your values remain fairly stable, your priorities may change as situations change and the meanings of the moment—by definition—undergo constant changes. It is wise to keep in mind Frankl's emphasis on the "defiant power of the spirit," which enables you to take a stand even against widely accepted values, and even against values that you have lived by for a long time. A stand against accepted values, however, should be taken only in new and extraordinary circumstances, never lightly.

Homework

Write your credo—your basic beliefs about the meaning of life. Write it as a number of statements that begin with "Life is most meaningful when . . ."

Fifth Session: How To Deal with Critical Situations

Traumas and critical situations often result from conflict between:

- the way you want to be and your daily behavior
- your long-range goals and daily needs (physical-psychological) and your reactions to the meaning of the moment (noetic)
- your self-interests and your desire to do things for people you care about

Participants are asked to write down three examples of each of these conflicts. Here are a few:

- I want to be a potter, but I spend all my time cleaning house and taking care of my family.
- I am stingy, but I want to behave like a saint.
- I want to be a good husband, but I need an occasional fling.
- I wish I had more time to spend with my mother, but I have my own life to lead.

Such conflicts can be made at least tolerable when:

- You find out more about your real goals and ambitions and admit them to yourself, even if they are not socially acceptable.
- You begin to make changes in yourself that could lead to achievement of your long-range goals.
- You empathize with another person.

Again, the participants form small groups. Use material you have written during the previous sessions and as homework as the basis for discussion of changes that you might be able to make in the ways described by the three statements above. Take one conflict situation that is bothering you now, and see how you could improve that conflict by approaching it with one of these three perspectives. Listen to the feedback from the others in your group, and see if it can help you to develop a new behavior pattern that is acceptable to you. Group members should not give advice. Instead, suggestions should be given in carefully worded forms:

A group member could say, "I was in a similar situation five years ago, and I know how it feels. What I did to overcome that crisis was ..." Another participant, using the "if I were you" approach, might say, "I have never been in such a situation, but I imagine that if I were I would ..."

Another approach is to "act as if"—as if you were the person you would like to be. This works when the conflict is between what you want to be (and what deep within you believe you *can* be) and the behavior pattern you have used for a long time. With small steps, and—at first—in safe situations, you begin to act as if you are the person you want to be. This "as if" behavior can be practiced in the group before it is tried out in the world. (See Appendix B.)

Homework

Consider why your life seems meaningful now, then list all the reasons you can think of. Select the five most important reasons and number them from 1 to 5.

List five situations in which, at present, you feel you are irreplaceable.

List five people for whom you are now irreplaceable.

Sixth Session: How To Deal with Meaninglessness

Existential despair can be the result of

situations you perceive as meaningless
your existential vacuum
a feeling of hopelessness, of being trapped

Write down in your notebook an episode that occurred more than five years ago that seemed to you to be meaningless. Discuss it with your group. What lessons did you learn from that experience? Has anything good come from it? How have you benefited from it? Looking back, can you now see any meaning in that old situation? Let the others in your group help you by suggesting possible meanings in that situation: What would *they* have found useful in that situation? What have they found meaningful in similar experiences? Share with your group the lists of people and situations with whom you feel irreplaceable, and discuss your feelings about the list.

Next, write down one situation in which you feel trapped right now. Make a list of all the choices you can think of in this situation, including the impractical and even the ridiculous. With the other members of your small group, discuss your lists and, with suggestions from others, come up with the one choice that seems most feasible to you right now.

Then, again with the help of the others, try to decide on a first practical step that you would have to take to realize the choice you have selected.

Now the helper talks to the group briefly about the principal thesis of logotherapy—that "life has meaning under all circumstances." This basic belief in the meaning of life can be understood as an awareness that, in spite of all apparent chaos and injustice, there is order in the universe, and that each individual is part of that order. Life makes sense in moments when you feel connectedness, unity—not only within yourself but also with the rest of the world. Such moments are rare and precious, and you must be aware of them as glimpses of meaning. In daily living, meaning is pursued through responses to the meaning offerings of the moment. You can find meaning in three areas: in your activities, in your experiences, and in your attitudes in situations that at first seem meaningless.

After this presentation of the basic ideas of logotherapy, the participants share the credos they have written as homework. Each person writes a statement on the blackboard, and then the group develops a shared credo, starting with the phrase "Life is meaningful when ..."

Homework

Pretend to be someone who is close to you. As that person, write a letter to a mutual friend or relative saying that you have died. In the letter, describe the kind of person you were, what was important to you, what difference it will make to the world that you have died, and what about you is most worth remembering.

Seventh Session: How To Deal with Depression

Depression can originate in any of the three dimensions—the somatic, psychological, or noetic—or in a combination of them.

A depression that originates in the body can be relieved, even if not cured, by medication. A depression that originates in the psyche can be helped through psychotherapy. Individuals with severe depression are to be referred to psychiatrists, especially to those who take into consideration the dimension of the human spirit. Logotherapists can work with psychiatrists and traditional psychotherapists to help depressed individuals. Logotherapists can use the four-step approach developed by Elisabeth Lukas.

The first step is to help the depressed person achieve distance between himself and his depression, to see himself—not as a person who is depressed but—as a full human being who has depressions but also the capacity to find meaning despite the depressions.

The second step is to help the depressed person to achieve a new and positive attitude—to use medication and psychotherapy to overcome the depression where this is possible, to learn to live with its limitations as far as it is unavoidable. The third step is the result of success in the first two steps—the depression becomes bearable, decreases, and may even lift.

The fourth step is a search, by the therapist and the depressed person, for a new and meaningful behavior structure. Practical ways must be found to structure the life of the depressed person—even during the depressed periods.

A depression cannot be denied, or wished away, or willed away. Telling depressed people to pull themselves together, or telling them that others are worse off, usually exacerbates the depression by making them feel guilty because they are unable to overcome their condition. Depression must be faced as a condition to be lived through and, when possible, overcome. Symptoms can be relieved by medication, and a change of attitudes can be achieved.

Here is one practical method for breaking your pattern of depression. Write down what you did the previous day, hour by hour. This recall will reveal to you that you were not actively depressed for the 24 hours of that day. Actually, most depressed people function normally part of the time. They cook breakfast, talk to the mailman, take the dog out for a walk, react to telephone calls and even to the little emergencies of daily living—they forget about their depression and function normally for short periods of time. These are achievements you need to recognize. How can you extend these periods of normal functioning? How can you find meaning in activities and experiences that take your mind off of the depression? Group members seek answers to those questions by listing the five ways in which meanings are likely to become conscious:

(1) learning the truth about ourselves
(2) having choices
(3) feeling unique
(4) acting responsibly
(5) thinking and behaving in self-transcending ways

Exercise

Participants are asked to write down a schedule of activities for the next day, and to relate those activities to the five approaches listed above. For example:

I have to get the children to school. (4)
I could stay in bed, but instead I will make breakfast for my husband and children. (2) and (5)
I will not phone my mother because that makes me more depressed. (1) and (2)
I'll surprise Sue and fix her pajamas. (2) and (5)
I'm going to visit Mildred because I know she enjoys my company. (3)
I'm going to play the piano because that makes me feel good. (1)
I'll go over to Peggy's house and help her prepare the party for Bobby's birthday. (5)

In the group, each person can make a list, and everyone can help by brainstorming—then the participants can adopt ideas from the lists of others in the group.

The exercise above is an application of dereflection, used to counteract hyperreflection, which is an excessive amount of attention to the self. Depressed people are encouraged to accept the tasks of daily living, and so to dereflect their attention, at least temporarily, from the depression. This is an example of Elisabeth Lukas' first step—achieving distance from your symptoms. When depressed people have experienced, in even small ways, that they are not helpless victims of depression, that they can take a stand against depression, then they recognize the power of the human spirit.

In cases of severe depression, the individual's noetic resources may be blocked. When working with such people, it may be necessary to arrange for medication or traditional psychotherapy to remove the barriers to noetic resources. But even people with severe depression may be able to accept simple dereflective tasks as soon as the dark cloud of depression begins to lift. Small changes in daily behavior can show the path out of what seemed to be an inescapable trap.

Homework

On small slips of paper, write a one-sentence note addressed to each member of the group. Start with the phrase "I really appreciated your being in the group because ..." Do not sign these notes.

Eighth Session: What You Have Learned for Daily Living

This is the last meeting of the group. What has happened to the participants?

For the last time, group members start the session by indicating where they are on the scale from 1 to 5. Then it is time to consider what has happened during the past eight weeks that has changed about where you are on that scale, and to think about what you can learn from the changes you have experienced.

- Write in your notebook, and share with the group, two things you have learned and two things you had not expected.
- What have you learned about your uniqueness? Write down and share five reasons why you would be missed if you died tomorrow.

The group leader collects the statements of appreciation that group members wrote as homework and distributes them to the participants to whom they are addressed. Then each person in the group has several anonymous statements about why his or her presence in the group has been valuable.

The leader encourages group members to continue to use the tools of logotherapy, to continue many of the exercises, and to continue writing in their journals (focusing on the five areas of meaning potential and writing on four levels—daily, weekly, monthly, and yearly):

Each evening, write what was meaningful for you that day, and what was meaningless. Each week, write what was meaningful for you that week, and what was meaningless. Do this exercise once a month, and once a year, recording what was meaningful and meaningless during the past month and the past year. Your individual pattern of meaningful and meaningless activities will emerge as you do these exercises.

You must learn to say goodbye, not only in the larger sense of relinquishing past periods of your life to which you can never return, but also in the smaller, day-to-day sense. To live in meaningful ways is to respond to the offerings of the moment, to live in the present while learning from the past and reaching for the goals of the future. To live in the present you must be able to say goodbye to meaningful involvements whose times have passed. The meaning of specific activities cannot be captured and held forever.

Example:

When you drive from work (which is meaningful from 8 A.M. to 5 P.M.) to home (which is meaningful from 5 P.M. to 8 A.M.), you need to switch your focus from one to the other. You may find it helpful to pull off the highway and park on a side street, where you can sit and meditate until you are open to the meaning opportunities that you are approaching. Then drive home to your family.

- What are the activities in your daily life that are most meaningful?
- What do you do to change your focus as you go from one set of activities to another?
- How do you say goodbye to one meaning before the next one begins?

During the last few minutes of this last meeting together, group members form a circle and stand holding each other by the shoulders. Each of you has your past, the notebook you accumulated during the sessions. And each of you has your future, the plans you have made to continue with the structure of finding meaning every day.

Now say goodbye, and get on with your lives.

Appendix B

The "Act as if" Method

The "act as if" method is used to build confidence in dealing with people. It enables you to translate wishful thinking into action. This method is not intended to persuade you to act as if you have qualities you should not or could not have. Rather, it helps you to achieve the personality you want and to realize your potential for becoming the person you want to be.

When you act as if, you soon come to believe that you are the person you are portraying. The only reason you have not been that person until now is that you have believed that you could not be, and so have acted accordingly.

When you start to use the act-as-if method, you must be prepared for an initial period—which may be discouraging—during which you have not yet begun to believe in yourself. During that period you will have to depend on the process to achieve belief in your ability to become the person you want to be. Remember that you cannot change your feelings at will, but you can change your behavior. Continue to act as if you are the person you wish to become, even if, at first, you do not fully believe that this will succeed.

This method can be most effectively applied by following five steps. Each of these steps requires only five minutes a day. Only one step is ever done on any one day.

Adapted from *Logotherapy: New Help for Problem Drinkers* by James C. Crumbaugh, W. M. Wood, and W. C. Wood (Nelson Hall, 1981)

Step 1: Alone

Begin in a completely nonthreatening circumstance, in which it will be almost impossible to fail. Choose a situation where, for the next five minutes, you will not be in contact with any other person. If someone should show up unexpectedly, stop and start again later when no one is around. (During each succeeding step, if the unexpected occurs, stop and start again later.)

A walk alone is a good time for this first step. As you walk, you are to think, feel, and *act* for five minutes *as if* you are the secure, self-confident person you would like to be, a person who would succeed at whatever you try, even though you may not yet have decided on anything to try. How would such a person walk? How would such a person carry himself? Swing his arms, or whistle? Look down at the ground, or hold his head high? For this five minutes, act as you think such a person would act.

The chances are that you will do this first step without any problems the first time you try, and that you will be ready for the next step the next day. But if, for any reason, you do not feel secure or comfortable doing this first step, repeat it again the next day, and again until you do feel secure.

Step 2: With a Stranger

Today choose, for a five-minute period of practice, a place where you will come in contact with some person unknown to you. A walk in a park where there are strangers can provide the conditions needed.

As you are walking, when you pass a stranger, *act as if* you are the secure, self-confident person you would like to be, the person who would succeed at whatever he tried. How would such a person behave as she passed a stranger? Pass by, without looking up? Look at the stranger? Exchange a greeting? Be this person for five minutes as you walk in the park.

If you decide to exchange a greeting, you may be rejected by the stranger, who may choose not to respond to you. And that might upset you. If that happens, repeat the step. The chances are that you will have no trouble with this second step. If you do, stop, and repeat it the next day, and until you are comfortable with this behavior in this setting.

If you are rejected and that doesn't bother you, you have already accomplished the goal of Step 2 and are ready to go on without repetition. But be sure that you are not rationalizing when you tell yourself that the rejection does not bother you—be certain that that is really how you feel. Do not defeat yourself by going on to the next step prematurely.

Step 3: With an Acquaintance

For this five-minute practice period, choose a place where you will come into contact with someone you know casually. Again a walk may be desirable, if you can arrange to pass someone you consider a casual acquaintance. Or you might go to your neighborhood library, or to a store that you shop at regularly.

Again, behave in ways that express the attitudes described above. How would the secure, self-confident person you would like to be act in this situation? Stop and chat, or just nod and keep going? If this step causes anxiety or any other difficulty, repeat it on subsequent days until you feel comfortable.

Step 4: With a Personal Friend

Unless you can conveniently contrive to meet a personal friend while taking a walk, the setting for the exercise may have to be changed for Step 4. If you have a lot of friends who live close by and you know when you can expect to see one of them on the street, then a walk can again be an excellent setting.

If the friend you meet is one with whom you are comfortable, you may feel secure during this step. But you are risking something, because you are now acting as if you are self-confident, and that may not be the way your friend thinks of you.

The object of this step is to confront those who know you with a new image of yourself, and to get them to accept that new image. This may take a number of days, during which you consistently play this new role. If so, it is wise to repeat the exercise with different friends on different days.

As you progress, you will find that any surprise your friends may show will probably be a pleasant surprise for you. When you assume a more positive attitude toward yourself, you will inspire a similar response in your friends, and they will treat you as a confident person. This will inspire you to act with still more self-confidence, which you will then express in your *acting as if*. And gradually you will stop acting—your feelings of self-confidence will be real, and your behavior will naturally reflect those feelings.

Step 5: In a Conflict Situation

The final step in the act-as-if method is to place yourself, for five minutes, with someone who is somewhat of a threat to you—someone with whom you have had some friction or conflict. Again you are to act as if you are fully self-confident and secure in your ability to handle this interaction in a satisfactory manner. You do whatever you think a secure, self-confident person would do.

When you can successfully handle this step, you have accomplished what you set out to do: You will have learned to believe in yourself as you interact with others, and you can then use that self-confidence in building relationships.

You may have to repeat this last step several times on several different days before you have fully achieved your goal. Even if you do feel successful and comfortable with the step almost at once, you should repeat it at least once to be sure that what you are feeling is accurate. You are likely, in future situations, to again encounter circumstances that will lower your self-esteem; when that happens, you will need to review and perhaps even to repeat this entire series of steps.

This act-as-if exercise can be of continuing value to you in maintaining the self-confidence you need to continue having successful relationships and encounters.

Appendix C

Personal History Form

Mr. Mrs. Ms. Miss _____ Age: _____

Address: _____ Phone: _____

Check one: Single _____ Married _____ Separated _____ Divorced _____
             Widowed _____ Number of times married _____

Children: Number _____ Ages of boys _____ Ages of girls _____

Education: Highest grade completed:
            Elementary school   6   7   8
            High school   1   2   3   4
            College   1   2   3   4   5   6   7   8
            College attended: _____ Degree: _____

Ages of older brothers _____ Older sisters _____

     Younger brothers _____ Younger sisters _____

Health of father _____ Health of mother _____

If either is deceased, give year and cause of death:

_____

What was father like? _____

What was mother like? _____

Describe yourself: _____

When you were small, what did you want to be as an adult?

_____

Courtesy of Mignon Eisenberg, Ph.D., Midwest Institute of Logotherapy, 520 N. Michigan Avenue, Chicago, Illinois 60611

What did your father want you to be? _____

What did your mother want you to be? _____

What was your father's main advice to you? _____
_____

What was your mother's main advice to you? _____
_____

What was your nickname in grammar school? _____

What were your favorite childhood games before age 9? _____
_____

What is your earliest childhood memory? _____
_____

What was your favorite childhood story, fairy tale, book, poem, radio or TV program? _____

How did the story go? _____

What did your mother always say to you (her favorite phrase)?
_____

What did your father always say? _____

If all goes well, what will your life be like five years from now? _____

What makes you feel most happy, loved, successful, and glad to be alive?
_____

What makes you feel most unhappy, unloved, depressed, angry, disgusted, etc.? _____

If you could change anything about yourself just by wishing, what would you wish for? _____

What famous person would you most want to be like? _____
_____

What is the best thing that has happened in your life so far? _____
_____

What is the worst thing that happened? _____
_____

How many more years do you think you will live? _____

What do you hope to get by attending this course? _____
_____

What do you most want to know about yourself? _____
_____

With whom do you get into the most fights? _____

What do you usually fight about? _____

What is your favorite song? _____

What is the most beautiful word you know? _____

What is the ugliest? _____

In your last letter to or talk with your children, what was your best advice?

_____

At your funeral, what will your friends say about you? _____

_____

If a movie was being made about your life, what would the title be?

_____

When you were small, to whom did you go with your biggest troubles?

_____

Why? _____

When you were small, what did the family usually talk about at the dinner table? _____

What is wrong with your life? _____

What can you do about it? _____

What would be the first step toward improvement? _____

How do you feel right now, while you are filling out this form? _____

_____

Appendix D

Value Auction

This "game" is used by logotherapist Mignon Eisenberg in her groups in Chicago. Each participant has $10,000 to spend. The money can only be used for the value auction. There is no point in saving it for something else. Every bid begins with $100 and can only be raised $100 at a time. The top bid is to be $4,000. Look over the list of values and mark down what you wish to bid on, and how high you are prepared to bid for each value you list. Your preliminary estimates are not binding, and you can change them as the bidding goes on.

The "auctioneer" is like fate—he or she may make errors, or decide unjustly—but the decisions are final.

List of values to be auctioned off

Value	Preliminary estimate	Actual bid
1. A good marriage		
2. Freedom to do what you want		
3. Power to rule over people		
4. Love and admiration from friends		
5. Unlimited chance to travel		
6. Self-confidence and a positive attitude		
7. A happy family		
8. Recognition of your worth		
9. A long and happy life		

10. A complete library for
    yourself   _____   _____

11. A fulfilling faith   _____   _____

12. A month vacation to spend
    as you please   _____   _____

13. Lifelong financial security _____   _____

14. A beautiful home in
    beautiful surroundings   _____   _____

15. A world without prejudice   _____   _____

16. A world without sickness
    and poverty   _____   _____

17. International fame and
    popularity   _____   _____

18. To understand the meaning
    of life   _____   _____

19. A world without corruption
    or lies   _____   _____

20. Freedom in your work   _____   _____

21. A truly satisfying love
    relationship   _____   _____

22. Success in your career   _____   _____

Questions to ask after the auction

Are you satisfied with what you purchased?

Why did you want what you purchased?

How does it compare with what you actually have?

What surprised you?

Are your expectations realistic?

How do you feel (and act) when you don't get what you want?

Are you angry at those who got what you wanted?

Are you angry at the auctioneer (fate)?

Would you make an effort, now, to get in your life what you got at the auction?

What would you have to do to achieve that?

Did you spend all of your money? If not, why? Did you save some of it for something? For what?

Would you have liked more money? How did you feel when you didn't have enough?

Did you spend your money fast and become frustrated when you didn't have any left?

Did you follow your preliminary estimates, or did you bid spontaneously?

Are you aggressive? Sure of yourself? Did you get what you wanted?

How much effort did you make to get what you wanted?

Did you plan well? How flexible are you?

What did you learn about yourself? About others?

Appendix E

Self-Appraisal

Who am I? (Describe yourself as you see yourself realistically.)

_____

_____

_____

Who does my family want me to be? (You may write a separate answer for each family member.)

_____

_____

_____

Who do I want to be?

_____

_____

_____

What are my potentials?

_____

_____

_____

What are my obstacles?

_____

_____

_____

What can I do to realize my potentials?

_____

_____

_____

What would the first step be?

_____

_____

_____

What can I do to overcome my obstacles?

_____

_____

_____

What would the first step be?

_____

_____

_____

Appendix F

Purpose in Life (PIL) Test

This test, developed by James C. Crumbaugh, Ph.D., and Leonard T. Maholick, M.D., measures how much meaning you see in your life at the present. Answer each question on a scale of 1 to 7. The answers to the 20 questions will give you 20 numbers. Add those numbers. You will get a total between a minimum of 20 and a maximum of 140. A score of 92 or less shows a low meaning orientation. A score of 112 or more shows definite meaning and purpose in life. A score between 92 and 112 shows uncertainty. Take the PIL test once a month while doing the exercises in *Guideposts to Meaning*, and you will discover a trend in your meaning orientation.

The entire PIL test, which includes two additional parts, is copyrighted by Psychometric Affiliates and can be ordered, with its manual, from the Institute of Logotherapy, P.O. Box 156, Berkeley, CA 94704. The cost is $4.75 for 25 tests without the manual, and $4.00 for two tests and one manual.

1. I am usually:

1	2	3	4	5	6	7
completely bored			(neutral)			exuberant, enthusiastic

2. Life to me seems:

7	6	5	4	3	2	1
always exciting			(neutral)			completely routine

3. In life I have:

1	2	3	4	5	6	7
no goals or aims at all			(neutral)			very clear goals and aims

4. My personal existence is:

1	2	3	4	5	6	7
utterly meaningless without purpose			(neutral)			very purposeful and meaningful

5. Every day is:

7	6	5	4	3	2	1
constantly new and different			(neutral)			exactly the same

6. If I could choose, I would:

1	2	3	4	5	6	7
prefer never to have been born			(neutral)			like nine more lives just like this one

7. After retiring, I would:

7	6	5	4	3	2	1
like to do some of the exciting things I have always wanted to do			(neutral)			loaf completely for the rest of my life

8. In achieving life goals, I have:

1	2	3	4	5	6	7
made no progress whatever			(neutral)			progressed to complete fulfillment

9. My life is:

1	2	3	4	5	6	7
empty except for dispair			(neutral)			filled with exciting good things

10. If I should die today, I would feel that my life has been:

7	6	5	4	3	2	1
very worthwhile			(neutral)			completely worthless

11. In thinking of my life, I:

1	2	3	4	5	6	7
often wonder why I exist			(neutral)			always see a reason for being here

12. As I view the world in relation to my life, the world:

1	2	3	4	5	6	7
completely confuses me			(neutral)			fits meaningfully with my life

13. I am a:

1	2	3	4	5	6	7
very irresponsible person			(neutral)			very responsible person

14. Concerning man's freedom to make his own choices, I believe man is:

7	6	5	4	3	2	1
absolutely free to make all life choices			(neutral)			completely bound by limitations of heredity and environment

15. With regard to death, I am:

7	6	5	4	3	2	1
prepared and unafraid			(neutral)			unprepared and frightened

16. With regard to suicide, I have:

1	2	3	4	5	6	7
thought of it seriously as a way out			(neutral)			never given it a thought

17. I regard my ability to find meaning, purpose, or mission in life as:

7	6	5	4	3	2	1
very great			(neutral)			practically nonexistent

18. My life is:

7	6	5	4	3	2	1
in my hands and I am in control of it			(neutral)			out of my hands and controlled by external factors

19. Facing my daily tasks is:

7	6	5	4	3	2	1
a source of pleasure and satisfaction			(neutral)			a painful and boring experience

20. I have discovered:

7	6	5	4	3	2	1
no mission or purpose in life			(neutral)			clear-cut goals and a satisfying life purpose

Appendix G

Seeking of Noetic Goals (SONG) Test

This test, developed by James C. Crumbaugh, Ph.D., measures the strength of your motivation to find meaning and purpose in life. For each of the following statements, circle the number that most nearly represents your true feeling. Add up the twenty circled numbers. If your total is 73 or less, you are not very motivated to find meaning. If your score is 87 or more, you are definitely motivated. A score between 73 and 87 shows uncertainty.

The SONG test, copyrighted by Psychometric Associates, is available with manual from the Institute of Logotherapy, P.O. Box 156, Berkeley, California 94704. The cost is $4.75 for 25 tests without the manual, and $4.00 for two tests and one manual."

1. I think about the ultimate meaning of life:

1	2	3	4	5	6	7
Never	Rarely	Occasionally	Sometimes	Often	Very Often	Constantly

2. I have experienced the feeling that I am destined to accomplish something important, but I cannot quite put my finger on just what it is:

1	2	3	4	5	6	7
Never	Rarely	Occasionally	Sometimes	Often	Very Often	Constantly

3. I try new activities or areas of interest, and then these soon lose their attractiveness:

7	6	5	4	3	2	1
Constantly	Very Often	Often	Sometimes	Occasionally	Rarely	Never

4. I feel that some element that I can't quite define is missing from my life:

1	2	3	4	5	6	7
Never	Rarely	Occasionally	Sometimes	Often	Very Often	Constantly

5. I am restless:

7	6	5	4	3	2	1
Constantly	Very Often	Often	Sometimes	Occasionally	Rarely	Never

6. I feel that the greatest fulfillment of my life lies in the future:

7	6	5	4	3	2	1
Constantly	Very Often	Often	Sometimes	Occasionally	Rarely	Never

7. I hope for something exciting in the future:

1	2	3	4	5	6	7
Never	Rarely	Occasionally	Sometimes	Often	Very Often	Constantly

8. I daydream of finding a new place for my life and a new identity:

1	2	3	4	5	6	7
Never	Rarely	Occasionally	Sometimes	Often	Very Often	Constantly

9. I feel the lack of—and a need to find—a real meaning and purpose in my life:

7	6	5	4	3	2	1
Constantly	Very Often	Often	Sometimes	Occasionally	Rarely	Never

10. I think of achieving something new and different:

1	2	3	4	5	6	7
Never	Rarely	Occasionally	Sometimes	Often	Very Often	Constantly

11. I seem to change my main objective in life:

1	2	3	4	5	6	7
Never	Rarely	Occasionally	Sometimes	Often	Very Often	Constantly

12. The mystery of life puzzles and disturbs me:

7	6	5	4	3	2	1
Constantly	Very Often	Often	Sometimes	Occasionally	Rarely	Never

13. I feel in need of a "new lease on life":

7	6	5	4	3	2	1
Constantly	Very Often	Often	Sometimes	Occasionally	Rarely	Never

14. Before I achieve one goal, I start out toward a different one:

1	2	3	4	5	6	7
Never	Rarely	Occasionally	Sometimes	Often	Very Often	Constantly

15. I feel the need for adventure and "new worlds to conquer":

7	6	5	4	3	2	1
Constantly	Very Often	Often	Sometimes	Occasionally	Rarely	Never

16. Over my lifetime I have felt a strong urge to find myself:

1	2	3	4	5	6	7
Never	Rarely	Occasionally	Sometimes	Often	Very Often	Constantly

17. On occasion I have thought that I had found what I was looking for in life, only to have it vanish later:

1	2	3	4	5	6	7
Never	Rarely	Occasionally	Sometimes	Often	Very Often	Constantly

18. I have been aware of an all-powerful and consuming purpose toward which my life has been directed:

7	6	5	4	3	2	1
Constantly	Very Often	Often	Sometimes	Occasionally	Rarely	Never

19. I have sensed a lack of a worthwhile job to do in life:

1	2	3	4	5	6	7
Never	Rarely	Occasionally	Sometimes	Often	Very Often	Constantly

20. I have felt a determination to achieve something far beyond the ordinary:

7	6	5	4	3	2	1
Constantly	Very Often	Often	Sometimes	Occasionally	Rarely	Never

---

Reprinted with permission of Psychometric Affiliates, Murfreesboro, Tennessee

Appendix H

SOCIAL READJUSTMENT RATING SCALE

Each event that we experience can be rated in "life crisis units." The table below lists such events, ranks them from 1 to 43, and gives a value for each event.

Add up the values of life crisis units for events you have experienced during the past two years. You can then rate your score according to the following scale:

150 to 199	Mild life crisis (33% chance of illness)
200 to 299	Moderate life crisis (50% chance of illness)
300 and higher	Major life crisis (80% chance of illness)

Some of the events listed below can be avoided or postponed. It is advisable to plan your life so that you do not accumulate more than 150 points at any one time.

Rank	Life Event	Life Crisis Units
1	Death of spouse	100
2	Divorce	73
3	Marital separation	65
4	Jail term	63
5	Death of close family member	63
6	Personal injury or illness	53
7	Marriage	50
8	Fired at work	47
9	Marital reconciliation	45

10	Retirement	45
11	Change in health of family member	44
12	Pregnancy	40
13	Sex difficulties	39
14	Gain of new family member	39
15	Business readjustment	39
16	Change in financial status	38
17	Death of a close friend	37
18	Change to a different line of work	36
19	Change in number of arguments with spouse	35
20	Mortgage over $25,000	31
21	Foreclosure of mortgage or loan	30
22	Change in responsibilities at work	29
23	Son or daughter leaving home	29
24	Trouble with in-laws	29
25	Outstanding personal achievement	28
26	Wife begins or stops working	26
27	Begin or end school	26
28	Change in living conditions	25
29	Revision of personal habits	24
30	Trouble with boss	23
31	Change in work hours or conditions	20
32	Change in residence	20
33	Change in school	20
34	Change in recreation	20
35	Change in church activities	19
36	Change in social activities	18
37	Mortgage or loan less than $25,000	17
38	Change in sleeping habits	16
39	Change in number of family get-togethers	15
40	Change in eating habits	15
41	Vacation	13
42	Christmas	12
43	Minor violation of the law	11

[1] Reprinted with permission of *Journal of Psychometric Research*, V(11), Holmes and Rahe, "Social Readjustment Rating Scale," copyright 1967, Pergamon Journals, Ltd.

April 30, 1988

Rank	Life Event	Life Crisis Units

Rank	Life Event	Life Crisis Units

Rank	Life Event	Life Crisis Units

Reading List

James C. Crumbaugh, *Everything to Gain: A Guide to Self-Fulfillment through Logoanalysis*. Berkeley, CA: Institute of Logotherapy Press, 1973. $9.95

—————————, *Logotherapy: New Help for Problem Drinkers*. Chicago: Nelson-Hall, 1981. $17.95

Joseph B. Fabry, *The Pursuit of Meaning*. Berkeley, CA: Institute of Logotherapy Press, 1980. $7.95

Viktor E. Frankl, *Man's Search for Meaning*. New York: Washington Square Press, 1970. $3.95

—————————, *The Will to Meaning*. New York: New American Library, 1969. $6.96

Elisabeth Lukas, *Meaningful Living*. New York: Grove Press, 1984. $8.95

—————————, *Meaning in Suffering*. Berkeley, CA: Institute of Logotherapy Press, 1986. $7.95

All these books may be ordered from the
Institute of Logotherapy, P.O. Box 156, Berkeley, CA 94704

Special Offer

$2 discount when ordering New Harbinger Books
or cassette tapes using the coupon on this page

You get $2 off the total price when ordering from the list of books below (with a full money back guarantee). Or send for our complete catalogue of books and tapes and get the same $2 discount on orders made from the catalogue.

The Relaxation & Stress Reduction Workbook, $12.50 paperback, $22.50 hardcover

Thoughts & Feelings: The Art of Cognitive Stress Intervention, $11.50 paperback, $21.50 hardcover

Messages: The Communication Book, $10.95 paperback, $19.95 hardcover

The Divorce Book, $10.95 paperback, $19.95 hardcover

The Critical Years: A Guide for Dedicated Parents, $9.95 paperback, $19.95 hardcover

Hypnosis for Change: A Manual of Proven Hypnotic Techniques, $10.95 paperback, $20.95 hardcover

The Better Way to Drink: Moderation & Control of Problem Drinking, $10.95 paperback

The Deadly Diet: Recovering from Anorexia & Bulimia, $10.95 paperback, $19.95 hardcover

Self-Esteem, $10.95 paperback, $19.95 hardcover

Beyond Grief, $10.95 paperback, $19.95 hardcover

Chronic Pain Control Workbook, $12.50 paperback, $19.95 hardcover

Rekindling Desire, $10.95 paperback, $19.95 hardcover

Life Without Fear: Anxiety and Its Cure, $9.95 paperback, $19.95 hardcover

---

___ Please send me a free catalogue of your books and tapes. By using this coupon I will be entitled to a $2 discount on orders made from the catalogue.

___ Please send to me the following book(s). Enclosed is my check.

	Price
_____	_____
_____	_____
_____	

Name _____   less $2 discount   -$2.00

Address _____   sales tax if Calif. res.   _____

_____   shipping/handling   1.25

                                     total   _____

Send to: New Harbinger Publications, Department B, 5674 Shattuck Ave., Oakland, CA 94609